Embrace

Your

Greatness

Volume I
Signature Collection

By
Dawn M. Harvey
And the Women of "Embrace Your Greatness"

Published by:
Unlock Publishing House
5887 Allentown Road
Camp Springs, MD 20746

ISBN 13/ 978-1-60702-094-3

Printed in the United States of America July 2008

Acknowledgments

We would like to first give all glory to God. Father, we give you praise for your Son, your grace and your love. You are so worthy to be praised. May we continue to walk in Godly counsel and serve you forever. There is nothing that we could ever do to repay you for everything that you have done in our lives. As long as we live, we live for you. With your continued guidance we know that through every trial we will prevail. We give thanks to our Lord and Savior, Jesus Christ. He is our pathway to the Father. We thank you Lord for your great sacrifice in and for the lives of your people. We thank you for the life that you have given us and the spiritual tools that have surfaced to aid us in our walk. We are the women who have decided to "Embrace Our Greatness."

We would like to thank our families and friends for their love and support. We only want to become who God called us to be so we can be a blessing to the lives of others.

We would like to acknowledge and thank Victor McGlothlin for the many tools and insight he has unselfishly offered throughout this special project. We Love You.

Contents

Forward   *5*

Forward

Embrace Your Greatness is a program God gave me after some very difficult times in my life. I found myself alone during some of the most trying situations I had ever experienced. God was my only help and refuge. It was His power that allowed me to look at myself and have the strength to change and grow into the next dimension. I have experienced brain, lung and uterine cancer. I have also faced abusive situations and battled depression. I have made a lot of mistakes in my life. And contrary to popular belief, you can start over. With God, you can change your entire life. My desire is that no woman has to go through that journey alone. I was lost but now I am found. I was confused but now I see clearly. God was my solution in every instance. He healed my pain, my problems and my past. He is true to His word and there is nothing, absolutely nothing that He will not do for us when we receive Him.

The words that you are about to read are some of the results of this program. This book is a sum total of the journey and life experiences of women who are not just talking about being free, they are living it. Here, you will find thirteen women who have dug deep into their heart and soul to heal what was ailing them. Proverbs 20:5 (NIV) says, "The purposes of a man's heart are deep waters, but a man of understanding draws them out."

The women in these chapters have discovered the truth about themselves in Christ Jesus. They have "Embraced Their Greatness." They have embraced the seed of greatness that has been hidden inside them. That seed of greatness was hidden in their childhood, past hurts and disappointments. No longer are they subject the lies of their past. They have accepted what has happened to them in their lives, forgiven themselves and others for every mistake and taken control of their destiny.

What we have realized is life is similar to falling and scraping your knee. Initially, it hurts when you fall. You could just put a bandage on the wound, but by doing so you are just covering up the hurt and pain. Often, in our daily lives, it takes more than just a bandage to ease the pain. We might need something that will help heal that hurt. We would need an antibacterial ointment to aid the healing right where it hurts. Our lives are the same way. As we go through life, we have so many circumstances that positively and negatively affect us. What we find ourselves doing is putting a bandage on the pain as a way of coping and surviving instead of allowing God to be our personal aid.

Inside this book you will find real life testimonies of women who have made a sincere decision to change their lives through the power of the Almighty. As you flip through each page you will laugh, you will cry, but most of all your heart will be changed. There are stories of failing forward, stories of triumph and stories of deliverance. You will find someone in this book just like you. The truth is that no matter what you are going through in life, you are not alone. You have more company than you could ever imagine. And what I love the most is that if these women made it, so can you.

The profound shift that has happened in the lives of these courageous women has allowed them to accept and shed their past, conquer their fears and forge toward their destiny. It is impossible to hinder a woman who is determined to succeed. Consider the definition of hinder: "To interfere with the movement, progress or development of something or somebody." Find a woman who has her mind made up and you will find a woman that is unstoppable. She will run you over to get to her destiny.

When we move life out of the way we can begin to see clearly. That is what has happened here throughout the pages of this book. We as women have poured ourselves out, only to be filled by God. All the issues that were delaying our destiny have been released and now it's time for you to hear what God has made happen for us. Why am I excited about you seeing the move of God in our lives? Because what God can make happen for another, He can make happen for you....AND MORE!

May God speak to your soul as you enter a book that will allow you to look at yourself in the mirror and like what you see. May you see miracles and blessings all the days of your life.

~ Dawn M. Harvey – *Pastor, Author, Entrepreneur*

"A trying journey can only result in a phenomenal blessing." — Dawn M. Harvey

No

More

Running

Nicole Lowery

I've been running for a longtime. Until this point, that's all I've ever known. My life has always been filled with running towards all the wrong things. To GOD be the glory because my running has now come to an end. I have teamed up with a group of women and together we are learning to EMBRACE OUR GREATNESS! These mighty women are the reason that I have grown closer to God and been able to tell my story of deliverance. See, before I met these wonderful women, I didn't think that I had been delivered from anything. In fact, I felt that God really didn't care about me. How could God love me and allow me to go through such terrible trials in life? Why did God want me to hurt so much?

My life from the beginning was full of hurt and pain. I wanted to run as far away as possible the hurt. I had to grow up fast because both my parents had a drug addiction. I tried to be a good daughter thinking that maybe my parents would love me more than they loved the drugs, but that did not work. So, I began looking for love in other places. By the age of 15, I was pregnant with my first child. By 18 I was pregnant with my second child. By 22 I was giving birth to my third child and was still running trying to find love, peace, and me.

In 2000 I thought I had met the man of my dreams. The first day I met him he told me I was going to be his wife. He also told me that when he looked into my eyes he could see all my pain. He said that he was going to release me from it. This man told me I would never have another sleepless night. He told me I wouldn't have anymore nights full of nightmares ever again. He told me that he was now the father of my children and they would have his last name. I can remember feeling so wonderful, like I was saved. I don't know what I was thinking, but as far as I was concerned this man could walk on water. I would do anything to have him and anything to keep him. I honestly felt like I would die without him.

In 2001 we were married. We didn't start with a honeymoon like most couples. He had to finish serving time in prison for assault on a government official. This should have been my warning sign. It was during this time that a friend of a friend told me about a business opportunity. It was an opportunity to work from home. I decided I would let one of the independent sales associates come to my house and talk to me about it. Once again, to God be the glory. That sales associate was Ms. Dawn Harvey. God will place people in your life in some crazy ways, but I know there was a purpose for the two of us meeting. God did not reveal that until years later.

My husband was finally released from prison and we were happy. We did everything together. I felt I had my storybook family that I always dreamed of. After a while, our happy life started to get rough. My husband claimed the town we lived in was against him because of his past, and we would never be able to get ahead in life unless we moved out-of-state. Life began to be even more difficult now. He had no job and all we did was argue. One night he went out with his cousin and when he returned, I woke up to his fist in my face. I had to go to the hospital. When the doctor asked what happen, I told him I was playing baseball and was hit in the eye. To this day I do not know why he beat me that night. To my surprise, later that afternoon he came in the room and talked to me as if nothing had happen. He started talking about how stressed he was and how he didn't like seeing his family go through rough times. He said we needed to get away, so I agreed to move to Baltimore, Maryland. I sent my three boys to stay with my parents in North Carolina for a few weeks, while we got housing and other affairs in order. I figured it would be all right to let the kids stay with them for a little while. I grew up around drugs most of my life and nothing ever happen to me, or so I thought. I figured they would be safe.

Soon after we arrived in Baltimore my husband found a job and a place for us. I regained the kids from North Carolina. I began to think that our problems would get better. We had jobs, housing, and the kids were back with us. I had even found out that I was pregnant. There was no stress. For a while our life was smooth. I was a well liked person everywhere I went. My husband didn't like that though. He began trying to make me stay inside all the time. It got to the point where I did not even work anymore. He would say that he was just protecting me. He didn't want anyone taking advantage of me. I didn't communicate with anyone in my family and I didn't have any friends. After a while, he wouldn't even let me attend church. Someone had told my husband that some of the sisters in the church had been mentoring me and telling me that I did not have to live my life the way my husband had me living. He was also using religion and twisting the words of the Bible to make me stay in the marriage and accept the abuse. See, when I would show up with a black eye and a bruised arm, my first excuse to my church sisters would be, "God wants me to be strong and help my husband get through these hard times. It's my fault that he beats on me. I should not stress him out so much because he is doing the best he can." The sisters would just look at me with sadden faces.

I was raised in a Baptist church. My husband converted to the Muslim religion 10 years before we met. Before my husband and I were married I converted to that religion as well. I depended on my husband to teach me the word instead of reading and learning the word for myself. Never convert to something for someone else. I made that mistake. I was not living my life for God in my own religious beliefs, so how dare I convert to another religion that I didn't know anything about. Because of that mistake, I ended up serving man, and not God. I thank you Lord for being in my life now.

By the end of 2002 my marriage was still suffering. We were still fighting. Only now my husband was doing more and more drugs. The abuse had gotten more brutal. It is on record that the police came to our home about 18 times in six months. I was so tired. I tried to get away, but he would find me and bring me right back. I would summit to all his lies of a better life and then I would go back. It is so amazing how women in my same condition will take beating after beating and still submit to their abuser, but will not submit to the will of God. God loves you and will not hurt you.

I was about five months pregnant and so tired of the fighting. One day I took the kids and tried to run away. We hid in my sisters-in-law laundry room. We stayed there for a whole day. She brought food down for us to eat. Just when we thought the coast was clear for us to come out, my husband showed up from out of nowhere. This time he used fear to bring me home. He beat me so bad that night that I could barely move the next day. Throughout the whole day, I bled off and on. I finally decided to go to the hospital. It was too late because I was not 24 weeks pregnant yet so there was nothing that could we could do. I felt the life of my daughter slip right out of me.

During this time my husband never left my side. I don't know if he felt bad about what he did or if he was just scared I would report what happened. I did not tell. I was so twisted up inside when I left the hospital because I knew I needed to leave him. In my mind, I felt like if I could get him off the drugs and into counseling, he would get better and love me the right way. I feared my husband in two different ways. The first way was fear of not being loved. I wanted to feel loved so bad. At the time, I didn't understand that if you didn't know the love of God it was impossible to love yourself. And if you do not love yourself, you can't receive love from anyone else. The second fear was of getting hurt or him killing me. Most days I didn't know if I was coming or going. For a few days he put as much fear into me as he possibly could. He told me often that if I tried to leave he would kill me and take the kids and no one would ever find them. A few days after my miscarriage, my mother and sister were in the area visiting, so they stopped by. I didn't get along with my family anymore but they all loved my kids. My sister and my mom took my boys out for the day. It turned out that they did not just take them out for the day; they took them back to North Carolina to live. Oddly enough I was relieved that they had lied to me. I knew the kids would be safe with my family in North Carolina. My husband thought I set it up for the kids to leave that day but I didn't. I now realize it was God that set that up.

My husband was so angry. He would look at me and start beating me. I prayed and prayed for God to take my life. I really wanted to leave my husband but I could not make myself leave. I don't know why. I figured if I didn't have enough strength to leave then I would rather die. A few weeks went by and one morning I woke up. My husband had gone to the store. I felt like someone had lit a fire underneath me. I called the police and told them I needed an escort to leave. I don't know what came over me, but I knew right then I was going to leave that house and nothing was going to stop me. When my husband got back from the store the police were pulling up. They escorted me out of the house and took me to the police station. My sister, who lived about two hours away, came to get me. For the first time in a longtime, I felt good. I had plans to get my life in order. One of the first things I did was contact an old business partner, Ms. Dawn Harvey. Looking back on the past, it is so funny how God works. Who would have thought that a business venture that started in 2001 would have given birth to a lifelong friendship, a church family and this book?

I called my business partner and told her I wanted to come back into the business that she had introduced to me to back in 2001. I told her about everything that had been going on in my life since the last time we had seen each other. She told me I needed to work on my personal development. She wanted me to build up my self-esteem and my confidence level. Ms.

Harvey gave me books to read as well as tapes to listen to. By December of 2002 I was with my kids and had a wonderful job that I liked. I even enrolled in a couple of college courses. I was doing well until one day out of nowhere my husband showed up. I knew I could not let this man back in my life. He said that he just wanted to help get me and the kids get settled in a place of our own. He said that he would help me get a car. Life was going good for me but my parents and I were beginning to have some issues. So, I decided to take my husband up on his offer. I believe I must have temporarily lost my mind. In less than 30 days I knew that I had made a mistake. See, I was not the same person anymore. I had grown. I had higher self-esteem and more confidence. I was reading my personal development books and I felt good about myself. I was happy with the direction I was going in life. I was even reading spiritual books that Ms. Harvey was sending me. One of my favorite books was the Prayer of Jabez. I know that when Ms. Harvey sent me that book she never dreamed that would be the book that would help keep me alive. I was not going to put up with the beatings anymore. I was better than that. I was starting to recognize that there is a God that loves me so much, He sent His Son down from the heavens to die on the cross for my sins. Do you know anyone who loves you enough to offer up their child to die for you and take on every sin you have ever committed?

During this period of time, I was beginning to love myself too. I did not need him to love me anymore. It did not matter. I told my husband I wanted to get a divorce. We were over. He agreed and we talked some issues out. I thought all was well.

On January 30, 2003 my husband walked into my house. I could see that he was on drugs. I didn't say anything because I was used to seeing him like that. He told me that he wanted to talk. He walked in the bedroom and before I could turn around he smacked me across the room. As he began to punch me, I could hear my kids in the background screaming. My husband yelled for them to come into the room. As I sat up on the bed I saw this shinny object coming towards me and then my back started to hurt. He was stabbing me with a screwdriver. He stopped and asked the kids "Who is your mom seeing?" They told him no one. In my husband's mind, if I wanted a divorce it must be because I found someone else. He kept asking the kids the same question and every time they did not answer he would drive that screwdriver into me over and again. The kids tried to jump on top of me to protect me but that didn't stop him from using more force with each thrust into my back. I had to turn over on top of my children so they would be out of harms way. When it was over he had stabbed me numerous times and when I finally arrived at the hospital the emergency attendants wiped away the blood and to everyone's utter amazement, the wounds that were visible were nothing more than deep punctures. The amount of blood that I lost did not match the wounds that were now visible. Based on the amount of blood I lost, I should have been severely injured. It is only by the grace of God that none of my injuries took my life. I had survived. I only received stitches. It is amazing; I felt that screwdriver going in and out of my body several times. I should have been dead or at least seriously hurt. That was the power of God. If the screwdriver had penetrated deeper, it would have hit major organs. It is by Gods grace that what should have killed me only bruised me.

You would think that after all of this drama, I would have given my life over to Christ and lived happily ever after. It was the exact opposite. Over the next couple of years my life was just full of chaos. God showed me His power that night I was assaulted in front of my kids. But Satan would not to let me go. The devil used many issues to trap me. It is not all his fault because often, I would place myself in the situation and environment. I lived my life lost and reckless. In 2004 I lost my daughter at the age of 10 months. In 2006 I delivered twins and lost one of them. I almost lost my life because of an infection from my caesarian. With everything that I had been through, hadn't I been punished enough? The enemy tried to make me believe that God did not love me and that He was punishing me. I asked myself on more than one occasion if that could be true.

In June 2007 I was invited to go to two day a women's conference called "I Am Whole" hosted by Dawn Harvey. I didn't plan to go, but my good friends Felicia White and Dawn Harvey were not going to let me miss this event. I went and this conference changed my life. I was sitting at the event listening to the testimonies of the women of a group called "Embrace Your Greatness" and like a freight train everything that I had been going through hit me all at once. God has always been there watching over me and protecting me and my family. It was God that was watching over me when my husband beat that baby out of me and did not kill me. It was God that was watching over me when I was running for my life and when I was stabbed. God told Satan you can't have my daughter. It was GOD! He has always been there for me. I just wouldn't sit still long enough to listen. He tried to get me to listen but I kept running. I had been running my whole life but the running stopped that day at the retreat. I gave my life to Christ on that day and I am now a new person. I asked for His forgiveness and accepted Jesus Christ as my Lord and Savior. After the conference, I didn't want to go back to how I used to be so I needed to connect myself with the right people and get the knowledge I needed by learning the word of God for myself. I joined "Embrace Your Greatness" and my life hasn't been the same. I am so thankful to God for placing these women in my life. I am walking into my greatness and doing the will of God. I want to walk in virtue and embrace Gods plan for my life. I wish the same for you.

Initially, I wasn't willing to revisit the pain and trials of my past. Then God delivered me from any concern about my life. I have buried this pain for over 25 years.

Revelation 12:11 says, "They overcame him by the blood of the Lamb and by the word of their testimony; they did not love their lives so much as to shrink from death." I keep going back to this scripture because it reminds me that as we walk in this life we make mistakes, but the enemy is overcome by our recognition and repentance of those mistakes. And others can be free by sharing our testimony. The enemy has no control of me and he can't tell on me because I am going to tell on myself. I am no longer a victim of my circumstances or past. I have been able to overcome my obstacles and I pray that you too, can do the same. Always remember to embrace life and the trials that come with it. It is in your trials that God is able to step in and perform healing and restoration for you.

"It is impossible to hinder a Woman who is determined to succeed." — *Dawn M. Harvey*

Change

Walterella McNear

In December 1997, after the death of my husband Ellison, I moved from Savannah, GA to Hinesville, GA. Ellison's tragic death occurred at the job where he worked as an Automotive Technician. Around November 1998, roughly one year after I moved and settled into my new life, I sincerely rededicated my life to Christ. It was such an intense spiritual growth. Something I had never experienced before. God is faithful when we are obedient to his word. I made a firm commitment to live a fully devoted, submitted life to Christ because I was so tired of just being a Sunday morning churchgoer. I had been doing that all my adult life. I was to a point in my life where I would feel like a hypocrite every time I stepped in the church doors. I remember the year 1996 when my late husband and I became members of a church in Savannah, GA. I tried to talk with my late husband about fully submitting to Christ and allowing Him to use us in the ministry. Even back then I grew tired of struggling with the guilt of going to church on Sunday morning and the next six days living outside God's will for my life. If we say that we have no sin, we deceive ourselves, and the truth is not in us (John 1:8). It was at that point, especially the last few months of my husbands' life that I was not feeling good about just going to church and just being a member on the attendance roll. I was convicted but my husband was not feeling the conviction and guilt that I was feeling. He was content with our usual church attendance. I could sense that he was still angry at God for the crisis he found himself in his previous marriage, before our union. My husband went through a fiery trial in that marriage and a sour divorce. He *healeth* the broken in heart and *bindeth* up their wounds (Psalms 147:3).

Now, I was raised in the church until I was about 14 years old, which is when I left my grandfather's house to move in my mother's house. My mother was an alcoholic and did not attend church. My grandfather cared for me from the age of 2 months old until I was 14 years old. My grandfather, Walter, was a deacon at our little country church back in Gary, Indiana. I don't remember ever missing a Sunday service or Wednesday night prayer meeting. My grandfather, Walter Sago, Sr., was a prayer warrior. When it was his turn to pray, my grandfather would pray so long and hard, at least back then it seemed like hours. Tell you the truth; I was always a little embarrassed because you could sense the congregation would get a little impatient because they were so concerned about sticking to the traditional program. I did not understand what was causing my grandfather to just go on and on praying, but now that I look back I can say my grandfather was bombarding heaven with intercessory prayer for many people. I know he was praying for me.

There was a season of my life that a spiritual transformation took place. In November 1998 my life transformed from a life of hypocritical living to a life of giving, a life of serving, and a life of living for Christ. I had made up in my mind that I wanted to devote myself to God in my heart, body, mind and spirit. If we confess our sins, He is faithful and just to forgive us our sins, and to cleanse us from all unrighteousness (1 John 1:9). I found myself tied to the altar every time I went to church. The altar call was one of my favorite moments and I would find myself at the altar crying out to God to change me from within, to change my life and make me over. I yearned for true submission to God. I felt so strong about staying on the altar to allow God to work on me and the vices that were in my life. To be honest, I started feeling this way in 1996, a year before my husband's accident. I wanted both of us to submit to God, and stop living the hypocritical lifestyle.

Yes, we were both saved but not living a submitted life to God. I can remember one particular Sunday, during the year of 1996 at church, when I decided that I was going to go up and be baptized again. I was baptized as a little girl. This particular Sunday, however, the urge to be baptized again was so strong on me. The Pastor announced it in the service and I decided on the spot that I would do it. It was a coincidence or so I thought that they had extra garments available. I asked my husband if he would join me, but he said he understood why I wanted to get baptized, however, he did not feel it necessary for him to get baptized again. So I got baptized and afterwards I felt such a comforting feeling in my heart towards God. I cannot explain it.

We left church that day after I was baptized and when I got in the car I began to cry and cry. My husband looked at me as if to ask "Why are you crying honey?" When he saw that I was unable to stop crying, he finally asked what was wrong. I was so distraught and unable to explain what I was feeling and experiencing at that moment that I couldn't talk. Before the discovery of the unfaithfulness in Ellison's previous marriage, he was very close to God, trusting God and faithfully serving in the ministry until he experienced a disappointment with the ministry that he was serving in. His previous wife and their pastor were cheating together and betraying him behind his back and they ended up marrying each other. This was a blow to my husbands' faith in God.

All of this happened a few years before we met and were married. My husband's faith crumbled after that ordeal. For when your faith is tested, your endurance has a chance to grow, so let it grow, for when your endurance is fully developed you will be strong in character and ready for anything (James 1:3). My husband loved God so he could not understand how God would allow that to happen. He expressed to me how he felt so betrayed by his ex-wife and pastor. After we married, Ellison would sit for long periods of time and discuss the entire ordeal with me, and I could feel he extremely upset with God. My heart would ache for him because I did not want him to blame God for what had happened to him. I really wanted him to love and serve God as he once did. I wanted him to forgive them, let it all go, and ask God to heal him of unforgiveness. For if ye forgive men of their trespasses, your heavenly Father will also forgive you. But if ye forgive not men of their trespasses, neither will your Father forgive your trespasses (Matthew 6:14-15). Ellison was emotionally bankrupt, but I could tell that he was a student of the bible. There would be times when we would just sit for hours discussing the word and he would nearly preach to me. He loved and knew the word of God. This was what impressed me about his character and the love he had for the Lord. I believe that he was called to preach, but after the horrible ordeal with his ex-wife, he lost faith in God to a certain extent.

I believe after we met and got married, a healing started to take place in him. It was a slow process for him though. However, a new burning desire for a true relationship with God came over me through my husband ministering the word of God. I believe we were connected in the spirit. I believe God connected us at just the right time. Before meeting Ellison, my life was in shambles. I had just come out of a bitter divorce myself. I was pretty much homeless, living with a Caucasian couple, in a trailer park in Walthourville, GA. I am forever grateful to them for taking me in during that devastating period of my life. I was spiritually, emotionally and financially bankrupt myself.

Nevertheless, I was surviving as best as I knew how. I was selling water treatment systems as a way to earn some income to survive. Before that, I was an Administrative Assistant for a large forklift firm in Savannah, GA.

Now, I don't believe there are any perfect couples in the world, but I felt that my husband and I were so perfect for each other. This was my third marriage and this time I felt it was a divine connection from heaven. Ellison's accidental death was such a horrific tragedy for me. I was in denial for a longtime after his death. Honestly, I began to believe it was a punishment from God. I, however, was not about to position myself to place blame on God for allowing that accident to occur. Eventually, through it all I found comfort and peace with God. Blessed are they that mourn; for they shall be comforted (Matthew 5:4). Some people come into our lives for just a season. There is a saying that has helped me get through tough times. It says: "Some people come into our lives and quickly go. Some stay for awhile and leave footprints on our hearts and we are never the same." Ellison will forever live in my heart and being able to experience the joy and the love he brought to my life has forever changed me. I sincerely believe all things happen for a reason.

I am now so aware that tomorrow is not promised to any of us so we should live each day as if it were our last. Ellison's life and death were a major influence on my decision to rededicate my life to Christ. After his death I relocated to Hinesville, GA and began searching for a new beginning. I began attending church, studying the word regularly and getting closer to God. As I mentioned in the beginning, it was an enlightening spiritual journey during that time. God was my refuge and I found strength in Him. I found myself desiring to hear the word of God more and to be in His presence every chance I could get. Initially, I believe I was trying to become righteous on my own and I quickly found out I could not control some of the habits I had on my own. I found out that prayer changes everything. I had not developed a prayer life because I did not know how to pray other than how I prayed when I was a little girl. You have probably heard the cliché "God knows our heart," but if we do not cry out to Him in a repentant state, and pray His word, we will fail every time at trying to give up sinful desires. I found that I had to sincerely cry out to God to help me change from the inside out. I could not stop the desire of listening to secular music, smoking cigarettes and drinking beer on my own. He that trusteth in his own heart is a fool, but whoso walketh wisely, he shall be delivered (Proverbs 28:26).

I've always loved music and I had been smoking and drinking since I was a teenager. When my husband passed away he was 43 years old and I was 37. So you see, I had a 20+ year old habit that I was trying to control myself and it was not working out for me. The temptation would come and I would succumb to it and afterwards, I would feel sick in my body and convicted in my spirit. My smoking habit was so out of control that I would say to myself I am not going to buy another pack of cigarettes and then later, I would not be able to resist buying a pack. I also went through having terrible headaches every day I discovered one day at my home, in my bedroom, the power of prayer. I cried out to God this particular day, praying His word and having a conversation with Him about my carnal ways and vices. This particular day I was so honest and open with Him, just as if he were my best friend. My prayer to God was a prayer of deliverance from temptation. They cried unto the Lord in my trouble and He delivered me out of my distresses (Psalms 107:6). Before I began crying out to God in sincerity, I constantly struggled with these vices. Therefore, to him that knoweth to do good, and doeth it not, to him it is sin (James 4:17). I had the desire to quit smoking, but I had no strength and I had not turned it over to Jesus. But be not thou far from me, O Lord, O my strength, haste thee to help me (Psalms 22:19). God is our refuge and strength, a very present help in trouble (Psalms 46:1). That was my prayer during these times. Every time I would light up a cigarette or drink a beer I would also get sick on my stomach.

Remember, during these times, I had not cried out to God for complete deliverance. I was trying to kick these habits on my own, specifically the smoking and drinking habit. When I met Ellison, I knew he was a Christian and my observation of him was that he was not a smoker. This was also one of the qualities that attracted me to him so I didn't want him to know I was a smoker. I tried to hide my habit for as long as I could. I would not smoke in his presence so I thought he didn't know. I had been smoking for so many years, that I did not realize that a nonsmoker can detect the odor of cigarettes on a smoker. Also, because he used to be a smoker many years prior, I could not hide my vice long. After we began courting for a few months, I decided to fire up a cigarette in his presence. Ellison confronted me one day about this nasty smoking habit and tried to convince me that I should consider quitting. He also shared that he knew I smoked from the beginning, because he smelled it on my breath and in my hair and clothes. I felt so embarrassed and sorrowful that I had even attempted to deceive him about my smoking habit. He showed so much concern, love and care for my health and well-being, that I tried to kick the habit even then on my own. It worked for awhile, but I was not totally delivered, I would still sneak and smoke my cigarettes and try to cover up the smoke smell by gargling with mouthwash, chewing lots gum and eating mints. Throughout the three years that we were married I never again smoked in his presence, but I would have my moments of weakness away from him.

What I do know is that when you cry out to God to help you in all sincerity and pray His word, He will deliver you from your vices. The bible says, "He sent His word, and healed them from their destructions (Psalm 107:20). I can put my name in the above verse. If you desperately want to be delivered from those vices don't let Satan keep you bound up; you are a child of the King and you too can receive deliverance. I suggest to you to cry out to the Lord, look to Him to strengthen you in your weakest hour. Deliverance is available to you.

Ellison shared his testimony of how he was once a smoker and had quit smoking many years ago. He said he would open the bible to study and try to smoke at the same time and it just was awkward and uncomfortable. Eventually, God took the desire away from him. That testimony has always stayed with me, because I thought that it was bold of him to try to study God's word with a cigarette hanging from his mouth. I wasn't that bold with my smoking habit.

I am saddened to say that during the last few months of Ellison's life, he developed the habit of smoking cigars. I'm still not sure how he developed that desire. I do believe it had a lot to do with the environment at work and of course, not being submitted to God. When he brought it to my attention that he liked cigars, I was surprised, but not upset that he enjoyed smoking cigars. I was still sneaking myself a cigarette now and then also. The habit was so strong I can remember the first day he went to the hospital after his accident occurred. He asked me to go and buy him a pack of cigars. He was craving them; however, because of his severe condition he was confined to the bed with tubes hanging everywhere so he was not able to leave the room at the time. So, I went bought the cigars and when I returned to his bedside with them. He fired up those cigars right there in the hospital room. I was so nervous, because I knew I should not have brought those cigars to the room and obviously there is no smoking in the hospital. It was late at night so he locked the room door and sprayed a lot of his cologne to cover the smell. I was so nervous, but I was feeling sorry for him because of the accident and pain he was in.

Ellison died on September 16, 1997. My smoking habit worsened and I was smoking a pack of cigarettes a day. In November of 1998, I made a decision to delight myself in the Lord and allow Him to give me the desires of my heart. Until I decided to give my struggles to God and cry out to Him in all sincerity for help, I was bound. I am honored to say that I have been delivered from drinking and smoking for almost ten years now. Remembering my struggles and victories helps me to keep in perspective who I am in Christ. My brothers and my sisters, here's a little prayer that helped me through my struggles:

"Prayer against Temptation"
Heavenly Father, How am I to resist these luring temptations
and live a godly, sober, fulfilled life with moderation? I don't
have to go far, search hard, or look long to find immediate
gratification, appeasement, comfort and satisfaction for my
flesh and carnal desires. Heavenly Father, I surrender to you,
and I ask you to take away these desires, and create in me a
clean heart and renew a right spirit within me. Help me, Lord
I believe that nothing should rule me or control me, especially
at the expense of my relationship with You, Lord. Please let
me look at the prize, which is a life of peace, fulfillment,
contentment, and completeness in your love and care. I
probably will not say these words when I am overtaken with
passion for self-gratification. I am saying them now, however,
so these words will prevail for me in my moment of weakness.
Give me the grace to stay focused and find the joy in your
wisdom and purpose for my life. Amen.

To all who read this, I pray that you will find strength and an encouraging word to help you make it through your journey of deliverance. So be enthusiastic, and earnest and burning with zeal and repent. Change your mind and attitude. There is hope when you put your trust in Jesus. He has given you the power to choose. I beseech you today by the mercies of God to present yourself to Jesus as a living sacrifice and choose to obey His word. I have refrained my feet from every evil way, that I might keep thy word (Psalm 119:101). Watch and pray that ye enter not into temptation: the spirit is indeed willing, but the flesh is weak (Matthew 26:41).

Thank you Pastor Dawn for a program that has allowed me to become what was already inside of me. I have "Embraced My Greatness". May God continue to bless you for your sacrifice and the time you spent with us.

Enough

Lillian Carter

It was nine years ago that I was a happy woman. Well, at least I thought I was. I was about to become a wife, would be moving to a new home and my finances were coming together. I was about to finish college. Life was just good. Although I had a sense of peace at this time in my life, I was not prepared for the devastation that was about to shake my world. I began to feel like life had dealt me another bad hand. I could not figure out what happened because this was supposed to be different. I prayed about it and everything appeared to be going right. Oh, was I wrong.

Here I was, in love and excited about my future. I never did choose the man; the man chose me, and with no apprehension. I was happy because this time I had a man who was already in church. I began pressing full steam ahead with my wedding plans. I had the engagement ring on my finger, the date picked out on the calendar, the colors were chosen, the dress purchased and over $4,000.00 spent. Yes, I noticed the stares, the whispers that didn't stop and people who wouldn't stop talking as well as plotting. I even knew about Ms. "Thang" who tried to stir up confusion in my life by calling me with the bad news. Well, to me none of that mattered. God would be pleased and the love we shared was like no other. I understood that love was supposed to conquer all things.

It wasn't until later that I realized that it was all a charade. For when he popped the magical question, he never expected me to say yes. Instead of backing away he chose to create a mess. In creating this mess emotional wounds opened. These were wounds that had not healed. This was major and it did some real damage to my heart. My heart shattered. The pain I felt was too much for me to bear.

I got the worse call I could have ever received in my life that day. I just don't know why someone would want to give me bad news and then act as if it wasn't a big deal. With all that I was going through, it was difficult to believe the Ms. "Thang" that I mentioned earlier had done all this for my benefit. If she really cared, why would she deliver such sad news over the phone? Did she even take the time to even think about how this would affect me? She didn't think about it because if she did then she would have been there with me, giving me her shoulder to lean on. Instead what she gave me was a slap in my face without even a second thought. Was this really a friend or what? On the inside I was angry with her, but I had to subdue that anger for the moment. I had more pressing issues that needed to be dealt with.

During this time, my favorite cousin was there trying to help me make sense of the whole ordeal. I did not want to believe what I was hearing. It could not be true. Why would he, my future husband, intentionally want to hurt me? I had been good to that man. I never tried to hurt, use or mistreat him. Even though my cousin and mother tried to console me, it just made matters worse. I had to get out of the house and do something to occupy my mind. I just couldn't stand to sit there any longer, so without any warning I got in my car and left. As I think back on it, that was the craziest thing I could have done, especially since I can't stand driving at night. I didn't even know where I was going. My head was hurting so I know I was not thinking straight. Through the tears and blurred vision I kept on driving and eventually reached my destination. Now that I was there what was I going to do? Although I acted on instinct and drove all the way over there, I was not prepared for what would happen next.

I saw both of his cars in her driveway, so it wasn't as if he was just visiting. He was living with her. Wait, wasn't he engaged to me? In my mind, something just wasn't right with this picture. You would have thought that I would have stopped right there since I had all the evidence I needed, but not me. I needed to have all my questions answered. So, I bravely knocked on the front door. When the door opened, there he stood without a shirt on and in his pajama bottoms. He then told me to go away. I instantly began thinking "the nerve of him, how dare he." At that moment I felt betrayal and anger raging up inside me. I began to scream "Why? Why did you do this to me?" Instead of answering me he just stood there. He had no answers and no explanation, not even an apology. Then he had the nerve to want me to go away. He must have been crazy if he thought it was going to be that easy. He must not have known who he was messing with. I was hurt, but I mustarded up all the strength I had left in me and pointed my finger at him and said, "You're gonna pay for this mess you've created." At that point I wanted to hurt him physically and I wanted him to feel the hurt I was hurting. As I went through this, I had to ask God to help me through it. It opened some wounds of rejection. This rejection was because of years of anger.

I thought that this would be the healing to all my years of being hurt and the hurt that left so much anger build up inside. I was happy that I was getting married. I was nicer to people and I didn't even snap at people when they said negative things about my relationship. I just smiled and fussed about it later. Now, because of what he did to me, I was again faced with rejection, embarrassment, feeling mistreated and misused. The fact that the man that I was to marry had moved in with another woman while he was still engaged to me just blew my mind. The thing that eased my pain had become another source of pain. How could four letter word called "love" cause so much pain? I felt like I was right back where I started; playing the defense.

So I began to send the notice out, "Do NOT mess with me." I guess some people decided to ignore it. They thought the embarrassment of not getting married had made me weak. They must have been crazy. I was about to shut it down. I was taking any prisoners and no one was free from my wrath. If you decided to step, then I STOMPED. When I finished, everyone would know not to bother that woman, she's crazy. The bottom line was I meant what I said, and said what I meant. I was determined not to ever get hurt again by anyone.

It's important that you understand that my anger was not new, it began when I was a child. I didn't know the scars, the rejection, the feelings of being unloved and unwanted would play such a huge role in the way I thought and acted. Until about nine months ago my anger remained buried and well tucked away. People who began to get to know me would have never known how bitter I was inside.

My mother probably never realized the hurt I was feeling inside. Perhaps maybe my world would have been different if I only told her. I didn't know how to tell my mother because I didn't think she loved me. I realize now, feeling unloved was the feeling of emptiness talking. I tell you, it was hard being the oldest and the only girl, but I managed. The hardest part was growing up in a home where my brothers had a father, and I didn't. Life was good for my mother as well. She was married, and the father of her two sons was still with her. You could say we were the perfect little happy family. I assumed that I was just a part of the package so that's why I got to stay. Even though I was there, I felt like I didn't belong, and it appeared my mother resented me because I was not a part of her happiness. I was just a sad reminder of her past. In my mind this explained why she was so hard on me. All I wanted was for my mother to love me. Instead I got the love I wanted from my granddaddy who just adored me. I became angry whenever she tried to interfere when my beloved granddaddy wanted to do things for me. It was no doubt in my mind that he loved me. Even after my granddaddy died, I would get in trouble when I asked for something. Why didn't she understand that I felt like the only person who loved me was gone? Who was going to love me now?

My negative feelings and resentment toward my mother played a major part in how I perceived my life. The "inner me" needed for my mother to love me so much more than she did. Instead I felt like I had to fight for the love I needed and wanted from her. Everyone else seemed to get my mother's attention and everyone else got her help. I, on the other hand, always had to do things on my own. It was almost as if what I did or needed was not important. After a while I began to act as if I didn't need her. I became private and would not let her in. There were many times when I needed or wanted my mother to be a part of what was going on with me but I just didn't want to cause her any pain or embarrassment. I felt like being born was embarrassment enough. I also believed that she did something to chase my natural father away. I never heard her say anything about him or mention him in her conversations. I can't remember my mother ever even saying, "You act just like your father." She never even said that I looked like him either. It was as if he didn't exist.

So all those years I kept my feelings and doubts locked up inside hoping one day the pain would go away. It wasn't easy because there were a few people who tried to play the role of being a mother to me and that didn't work for me. I used my anger to keep them away. I was getting good at keeping people away from me and out of my business.

It was not until the day after Thanksgiving in 2006 the opportunity presented itself for me to confront my mother. I blurted out, "Mama I've always felt like you didn't love me like you loved my brothers." There was no response and the conversations around us continued. "Perhaps it was true," I thought. I began to panic and didn't know what to say or do. Finally, my mother stopped the conversation which was still going, and said to me, "Baby, I do love you, just as much as I love your brothers." From that magical moment, and the rest of the conversation, I had no doubt that my mother did love me. I felt in my heart that it was never her plan to hurt me. This was such a huge relief, and it felt good to finally let it go. The love I needed and wanted from my mom was now available for me. I thank you Father, for interceding and bringing me and my mom together.

The sad thing was, even with everything that had happened; there was still one more thing that needed to be resolved before I would know that I was finally free. It was now time to deal with the anger and the bitterness that I felt inside for my biological father for deserting me. It was hard and painful because I was mad. I didn't deserve to go through it. The biggest question for me, which I likely will never get an answer to, was WHY? I have never been able to understand why he didn't even have the decency to wait until I was born to see if I were his child; even if he did have doubts. Not only did he rob me of him, but I was also robbed of not having the opportunity of knowing anyone in my father's family. I often wondered if he even told his family about me, or if they too rejected me. Typically, girls are spoiled by their daddies, but not me. It's sad because I don't know anything about him. I don't know if he is dead or alive, tall or short, good-looking, or if I look like him. I believe that a daughter should have a special love for her father, but in my case I was always so mad at him. I viewed him as a worthless man who ran out on his daughter. What a coward I believed he was. I bet he never realized that his foolish decisions would later have a huge affect on me. Sadly, I don't even think it mattered to him.

My father didn't understand that I was having a hard time trusting the males in the relationships I was in. I never wanted to date an older man in fear that he would desert me as well. My dad should have been there to protect me, to make those men pay for what they did to his daughter. Usually, fathers don't want anyone to hurt or harm their daughter. In my case, the man who impregnated my mother was anonymous. Now I see why my mother never mentioned him, for he had failed her as well. After awhile, my urge to have answers from my father turned into anger. I felt that just as I had wanted to search for him, he should have tried to find me because I was a part of him. I've tried for years to forget about what he had done, but with the hurt and pain of my last relationship ending the way that it did, it brought back all the feelings of anger I once had. And now it was destroying my soul. Amid all of this anger, I thank God for being God, and being my source of my healing. For not long ago God whispered in my ear telling me, "I'll never leave or forsake, I will be the Father you've never had." God didn't stop there. I know it was a part of His plan because He made a way for me, his daughter, to be able to help others. Surviving my pain has helped me understand someone else's pain. Thank you God for the journey I had to take, knowing that in the end you would work out.

I know now that my meeting Pastor Dawn Harvey was not by coincidence. It wasn't just for a business opportunity that our paths crossed. It was for a greater purpose. Father, I thank you for allowing me and other woman to take this class called "Embrace Your Greatness" at this appointed time, so we may truly "Embrace Our Greatness." The world will now see that having a personal relationship with God can change your life. So I surrender to say, "Not my will, but yours Lord".

What??

Your

Not

A Tither?

Maureen Whitsett

Heavenly Father, I want to first thank you for your merciful grace that you have shown to my family and I for the last 46 years of my life. I am humbly honored to be a part of a team of GREAT Women who have purposed in their hearts to serve you through healing and restoring the children of God back to YOU!

Exodus 6:5-8

5And I have also heard the groaning of the children of Israel whom the Egyptians keep in bondage, and I have remembered my *covenant.*

6Therefore say to the children of Israel: I am the Lord; I will bring you out from under the burdens of the Egyptians, I will *rescue* you from their bondage, and I will *redeem* you with an outstretched arm and with great judgments.

7I will take you as my people, and I will be your God. Then you shall know that I am the Lord your God who brings you out from under the burdens of the Egyptians.

8And I will bring you into the land which I swore to give to Abraham, Isaac, and Jacob; and I will give it to you as a heritage: I am the Lord. [Emphasis mine]

I became a Christian about eighteen years ago, and I have been saved for the last 10 years. I started off sowing financially but was not consistent. I cannot say that I was a tither because I found out in a teaching at my church that unless you are giving a tenth of all your income, you are not tithing. All you are doing is tipping God. See, I would give financially, but whenever an emergency would arise, I would tell God that I would give at another time. Most of the time I was able to do so but there were times that I couldn't.

My journey to becoming a tither based on the word of God started in 1996 when I sought out a company to help me to get out of debt. While working with this company I soon realized that owed the Internal Revenue Service almost $4,000.00. That didn't even include my normal day-to-day bills. In short, my finances were in a mess. That company eventually ended up going out of business. I was never refunded the money I lost while dealing with them. After seeking the counsel of a pastor I decided to enter a debt management program. While trying to get the balances from all my creditors, I ran into more trouble. One of the creditors that I owed money had been charging me late fees for several years. I had no idea these late fees were incurring. When it was all said and done I owed this creditor around $7,000.00. My check was about to be garnished. Before I found out this disturbing news I had been giving some thought to filing bankruptcy. I struggled heavily with trying to do the right thing. Finally, in October 1999 I felt I had no other way out so I filed bankruptcy

The year I filed bankruptcy I gave up my apartment to be able to put my finances in order. This included becoming a faithful tither. I struggled for a long time with my decision to give up my apartment. It was difficult to decide if I really wanted to give up my privacy and all the freedom that went with having your own place.

In 1999 my pastor challenged the congregation to tithe for 90 days or get your money back if God did not bless you. I felt the Holy Spirit talking to me when I agreed to tithe for those 90 days. I already knew God was faithful in the healing area. I had already survived third-degree burns over 65 percent of my body. While recovering from my burns, my children were taken from me and cared for by their father and his mother. Therefore, this caused me to have to pay child support. This was yet another expense. During this adverse time, I also had to deal with my children being told by their father and his mother that I was crazy. I have forgiven my ex-husband and his mother and Praise God because now I have the best relationship with my daughters. Despite what they were told during that time, we were able to get past that.

So I began my journey to fully trusting God with my finances. I am divorced but while I was married my husband handled the finances. After the divorce I had to manage my own finances. Because I had no experience in financial matters, it was a struggle.

I didn't realize at the time that all along the hand of God was moving. Things began to happen. I met with a wonderful woman of God at my church. Soon after meeting her I moved into her home. I lived with this woman of God for three years. At the end of the first year I had done a much better job of giving when it was time to give tithes and offering.

The First Lady of my church gave a sermon on living off less. That sermon ministered to my spirit. From that point on, I started being aware of my spending. Four years before this time the Holy Spirit was helping me and showing me ways to handle my records of spending. I would save every receipt and when the month ended I would categorize my expenses. I had been saving these receipts for a year or so before joining my church. After hearing that message about living off less, I pulled out those old receipts and the new receipts and began really analyzing my spending habits. What I found out was I wasting money and not asking God to guide me in my spending. My practices are much different now. I can remember talking with my oldest daughter in back August 2006 about some of the spending decisions she made. I looked up the words below in Webster's dictionary. I remember saying, you have to identify the following before creating bills or buying items:

- Needs – lack of something essential
- Wants – to have a strong desire
- Desires – to long or hope for

Well, the tithing journey continued for me. One of the pastors of my church was giving a testimony and casually stated that when you work for the church your tithes were automatically deducted from your paycheck. A light bulb went off! I did not work for the church but I immediately went to my bank the next day so my tithe money would automatically be deducted from my account and transferred to the church. This was a big step of faith for me. It meant that I could no longer tell God I would give when I could. I had to deduct my tithe from the gross before I paid any other bills because remember, it was an automatic deduction.

The year 2000 came and I was still having several financial challenges but I was beginning to see the light at the end of the tunnel. I was spending about $200 to $300 a month in car repairs. During this time the Holy Spirit moved on the heart of the wonderful woman I was living with and she helped me out by giving me her income tax refund check. I nearly begged her not to do it but she felt the Holy Spirit was telling her to do so. I thought for sure this was my sign to get another car. I could use the money to make a down payment, after I tithed of course. So off to the dealership I went. To my surprise I drove home with a better used car than I previously had. Within 24 hours I had to return the car because of my credit. God had to heal me from the humiliation I felt from having to return a car that I thought was mine.

The year 2001 came and the costs of car repairs were becoming overwhelming. I went back to my credit union just to inquire about getting a car financed. This had been my second trip because I was denied a loan to help buy the better used car the year before. The gentleman at my credit union said I needed to write a letter to the credit union committee. Don't forget I was in a Chapter 13 bankruptcy program at the time. The gentleman told me almost word for word what to say to the credit union committee. That was on a Wednesday.

He told me he would contact me by Monday with the decision. I then called a car salesperson from my church. I told him that my credit union committee was reviewing my paperwork and if they approved me, I wanted him to sell me a car. I explained my bankruptcy to him and he prayed for me. The gentleman at my credit union called me that Friday and said that I could go and look for a car that weekend. WHAT A MIGHTY GOD WE SERVE! That next week on February 6, 2001, I was pulling off the car lot with a 2000 Ford Focus.

The year before around spring of 2000, I felt the Holy Spirit telling me that He wanted me to stop taking classes at the University where I was working. I thought I was there so I could finally get my degree, but I kept feeling the Holy Spirit telling me to press into the things of God. In my natural mind, I did not understand how I was going to make more money without a degree. Still, I obeyed the Holy Spirit's prompting and put my classes on hold for a season. During this same time period I was going through some major challenges with my supervisor. My previous supervisor, who was a great man, resigned a year earlier. After doing all that I felt God was asking me to do in that position I cried before the Lord to remove me from that position. I felt I had nothing more to give.

About three months later a department manager approached me and asked me when I was going to give her my resume. The word was out about my gifts and talents administratively. I replied to her that I was going to consider her offer. Her reply to me was, "I wish you would." That afternoon I gave her my resume. God is so awesome because she created a position for me that included almost a $4,000.00 raise. I don't understand it but I know God's ways are not our ways (Isaiah 55:8). Before I started the new position, they asked if I would help out in another area in their department. The area that needed help was their business office. They needed someone to help pay the bills of that department. I took this challenge with much prayer because this area was new to me. I began to soak up all the training that they offered to me. After the training I transferred the knowledge the Holy Spirit had been showing me in keeping my own records for my bills. It was challenging because I did not have much confidence working with numbers, and it was a new field of work for me. A year went by and I asked to be considered for the position since I was already doing the job. HALLELUJAH!! I was approved for the position and I received $1,300.00 more a year.

On top of that, in June 2002 I went to settlement on my first new home. In November of 2002 I was officially discharged from the Chapter 13 bankruptcy program. PRAISE GOD!!! I was able to write a letter to the mortgage loan company to explain why I had been in the Chapter 13 program. After settlement, I felt that buying my home was the best thing that has happened to me in my life. Two weeks later, I was laid off from my job. I was devastated but optimistic in finding another job at the same company. I had an excellent work ethics reputation. Still optimistic, I signed up with several temporary agencies. Time went by and soon a year had passed. During this time, I was tithing from my unemployment checks. I was spending eight hours a day applying for jobs and going on interviews. I was selected on a couple of occasions to be in the top two of getting a job, but nothing ever came about. June 2003 came and my unemployment had run out. I had no money coming in. During this time, God had laid on the heart of several people in my church to help me out. One couple gave me enough money to cover my car insurance payment for several months. One sister gave me groceries from her home. A couple of sisters also gave me financial help. God was still meeting my needs even though I had no money coming in. I soon began working at a telemarketing company from 3:00 to 11:00 p.m. The job was a bit much for me because I had to adjust to the different hours as well as the new field of sales. I did the best I could at that job but left after working a month. My aunt invited me to work for her at her home-based business. She could not pay me what I was accustomed to making but nonetheless, I took the offer. To this day I am grateful to my aunt and thank God for her being the blessing that she is in my life.

In July 2003 I interviewed for the federal government and got the position. I accepted the position knowing it was a $10,000.00 cut in my previous pay. It was challenging because I still did not have enough money to pay all my bills. At my previous job I had borrowed from my retirement money which was a big mistake. Eventually I could not afford to make the payments so I opted to withdraw the entire funds from my retirement account to pay off the loans against it and to use the rest to pay off bills.

Well it's been almost four years now since starting that government job. All along the journey, God has been proving Himself to be faithful. God placed me in a department where the people recognized me and my hard work. I have another home, in a condominium community. I was challenged a little when I first moved in the condo but God blessed my finances. I was blessed to become acquainted with a person who has helped me develop a budget. I kept hearing people say that you should have a budget. I even enrolled in a couple of biblical budget classes. However, it was not until I started working this woman that I fully understood how to use a budget. What a blessing!

I'm here to tell you if you don't want holes in your pocket, I dare you to try God in giving your tithes and offering. As my pastor gave the challenge nine years ago, I challenge you to tithe for 90 days and see how God blesses you. It may not come back monetary but God could bless you with a reliable car, more money on your job, and a home to call your own.

More than cars, money, and a home I'm here to tell you that you will never be able to see, understand or experience the true blessings and promises that come with being in the Kingdom of God unless you have a covenant relationship with Jesus Christ (Romans 10:9-13).

Giving to the Kingdom of God is similar to a farmer sowing seeds of some sort to produce a harvest. I'm not a farmer but I did spend a couple of summers with my grandmother before she passed and helped her in her vegetable garden. When you put the seeds into the dirt, the seed could become a cucumber, tomato, or a potato. After cultivating the soil to foster the growth of the seeds you'll begin to see the seed bud and it will eventually sprout up into cucumbers, tomatoes or potatoes. When you give your finances or seed to the Kingdom of God, God supernaturally determines how your seed will sprout up. In sprouting up God will supernaturally turn your seed into health for your body, increased finances, salvation to you and your family, favor on your job, establishment of businesses, divine connections with relationships and an abundance of other blessings. Since God is in control and He knows the beginning to the end, He will determine what you need and when you need it. Trust God with your seeds and He will decide your harvest. Don't rob yourself or God from having an abundant life (Malachi 3:8-12). Thank you so much Pastor Dawn. You have helped me see myself and embrace my greatness. You mean so much to me.

"Do not allow your past to lie to you about your future."   *- Dawn M. Harvey*

Abuse,

Deliverance

And

Happiness

Felicia White

My story is based on some of the obstacles that GOD has delivered me from in my life. I don't think that I would have been able to share my testimony with you if it were not for Embrace Your Greatness. I joined Embrace Your Greatness in April of 2007. Embrace Your Greatness has allowed me to open up to other women of God and talk about things that have happened in my life. I didn't think that I would ever be able to share these things struggles with anyone because of what I thought people would think about me. Today I am grateful to have the opportunity share my testimony with you because Embrace Your Greatness has taught me that I am not judged but loved and destined for greatness.

It was the winter of 1999, in Smyrna, Georgia when I met the man that I thought I would spend the rest of my life with. We became close friends within the first six months of meeting. We were so close that I decided to introduce him to my two little girls. At the time they were ages three and one. After introducing him to my girls he fell in love with them. Then we decided to become a couple. We were very happy in the summer of 2000. We did just about everything together. I thought we were soul mates.

As the months went by, everything was great between us. We conceived our first child in the fall of 2000. We were excited about bringing a child into the world and raising this child together. We began planning and making changes in preparation for the arrival of our newborn baby. Amid all the planning and changing, he also started to change. He would get mad at the littlest things that I did or did not do. When he got mad he would break personal items of mine that were not replaceable. These were items that I considered close to my heart because they were given to me by family and friends. In April of 2001 he decided that breaking personal things wasn't enough to calm his anger so he began hitting me. I was seven months pregnant the first time that he hit me. After hitting me and leaving me doubled over in pain on the floor he left as if nothing ever happened. He returned later in the day apologizing for the pain he had caused and told me that he would never hit me again. We went to the doctor the next day to make sure that both the baby and I were fine. By the grace of God, we were just fine. The following June, I gave birth to a healthy baby girl. Our relationship was good for about a year despite the previous circumstances. We still had arguments that year but he did not hit me. It was when I thought our life was back to normal and we were back on the right track that he came back with a strong vengeance of hatred.

April of 2003 was the month that he went to jail for assault and battery and cruelty to children. He had come home from work on this day and was not in a good mood. I already knew that it was going to be a long night. He wanted to argue with me about anything and everything. It did not matter if he was right or wrong. When I would not argue back with him he decided to take it out on me in front of the children. When the police arrived at our home, he had already left. I filed a report against him. The next night the police took him into custody. He stayed in jail for three months. When he got out I was scared and even though there was a restraining order against him he still came to the house. He told me that he did not care that there was a restraining order against him and that he was staying at his house.

I had been praying to God for some time to help me to remove him out of the home that we were living in. See, at this point in my life I was sick and tired of all the fights, arguments and blows to my body. I just wanted to be free. Well, one particular day I was sitting on the corner of my bed and something was really bothering me. I could not figure out what had me so troubled. While I was sitting there on the bed, my mom and dad called and asked if I was all right. I told them yes and asked them why they would call and ask me that. They told me that they could hear the two of us fighting. My response to that was, "I'm not fighting with him." My mom then says, "Are you sure?" I respond with, "Yes." My mom then says, "This young woman sounds just like you on the phone." I say, "Mom, it is not me." Well, it turned out that he was fighting with a woman. He had been seeing another woman who was carrying his child. At the time, we were still together. The direct connect button on his Nextel phone had accidentally connected to my mom's Nextel, allowing her to hear their entire argument. At the time, this other woman was five months pregnant. I asked him when he planned to tell me that he had been sleeping with someone else and gotten them pregnant. His weak excuse was that he was not going to tell me because he did not know how. The truth was he didn't have to tell me. I was praying for a way out for a longtime and his unfaithfulness was my way of escape. That day was the day for me to become free.

When I put him out of my house in the summer of 2004 the enemy had me to believe that I was losing the best thing that ever happened to me. I became depressed, broke down and shut in. I would sit in the recliner rocking my baby on my lap feeling miserable and worthless. Even then, God had a divine plan in motion for my life. Months before all this drama and mayhem, I met a woman. I thought her purpose in my life was for a business opportunity, but God already knew that I was going to go through a breakdown. He sent me angel that showed up right at the point of my breakdown. He positioned Dawn M. Harvey in my life so she could help me breakthrough from the breakdown. She began to call me every day. Some days I did not want to answer my phone, but those were the days that she helped me through. She would pray with me and quote bible scriptures just to let me know that everything was going to be all right.

By the fall of 2004 I was going through the healing process. I was doing well. The girls and I were happy. During the winter of 2005, he showed up at my house. The baby-sitter allowed him into the home because she knew him and the girls said that they had not seen him in a while. I was in a business meeting when the baby-sitter called and said that he was there. When I got home he was still there. It seems that even though he was no longer living with us, he felt that he could still be in control of what was going on in the house. He was furious because I left the children with the baby-sitter to go to a business meeting. He did not approve of me leaving them with a baby-sitter. I disagreed with him. That's when he felt that he had to prove me wrong. While I was turning to walk out of the kitchen he had grabbed me by my throat and began squeezing breath out of me and banging my head several times into the kitchen cabinets. While trying to escape he ripped my clothes off my body leaving me broken on the kitchen floor. I thought that all the pain and hurt was over when I had put him out of the house the year before. I never thought for one minute that I would have to go through that again. It seemed like it was starting all over again. From that point forward he began stalking me. He would come to the house at all hours of the night and morning and bang on the door and windows for me to let him in. I got a restraining order against him but that didn't keep him away. He simply did not care about the words written on that piece of paper. He did whatever he wanted to do just to irritate me.

During the late winter and into the early spring of 2005 he calmed down a little because he wanted to see the girls. I allowed him to get them every other weekend. Sometimes we would meet at the police station just so there would be no problems. That worked for a little while until he felt that he should be able to pick them up from the house. So I allowed it. This went well with him picking them up from the house every other weekend. We didn't have any problems until one particular weekend in the spring of 2005 I asked him to switch weekends because I had a business partner coming into town. He said it was fine, so I didn't think anymore about it. Saturday came and the girls were gone. My business partner and I were finishing our meeting at my house when we realized that it was time to go pick up another business partner from class. So, as we were leaving I accidentally locked my keys in the house. Luckily I had my car keys, so we went to pick up our other business partner and then drove to my friend's house. She had a spare key to my house. When we arrived at her house she was not there, but as soon as we were getting ready to leave my children's father drove up behind us honking the horn. He came up to the window of my car fussing and yelling at me to step out of the car. He said he needed to talk to me. The girls were in the car with him and my two business partners were in the car with me. I figured with the children in his car and my business partners in mine and with a neighborhood full of people, he would not possibly think about hurting me. As I started to get out of the car my business partner grabbed my right forearm. She said "Please do not get out of this car; I am afraid of what he might do to you." I closed the door with him standing there fussing and yelling and drove off crying. I felt embarrassed that he would act like that in front of my business partners. I had just met these women for the first time in person. We had talked over the phone before but this was the first time that we were face-to-face conducting business and I felt that I had put them in harm's way. I thank God for understanding because they understood what I was going through. See, God will put people in your life that have already been through what you're going through so they can help you come through.

After the weekend incident he still wanted to be in control at times, trying to dictate what should go on in my house. He would still pop up now and then unannounced and bang on the door and windows trying to get in. He would make threats over the phone. He would always tell me that he would kill me. One summer day in 2005 he came to the house banging on the door to get in. I would not let him in because I already knew what was going to happen if I let him in. I had two friends staying with me just for the week, so my friend that was sleeping in the living room came to my bedroom door and told me that someone was banging and calling my name. I told her that I heard him and directed her not to open that door. She laid-back down and I stayed in the bed. We must have been tired the night before because we forgot to close and lock the front door all the way. When I was able to get out of the bed to go meet him outside he was already in the house telling us that he was getting ready to kill us all. When he went to the trunk of his car to get his gun I walked outside behind him. I told him if he wanted to kill me go ahead, but he was not going back into my house to take the lives of others. I was prepared to die that day. I just wanted all the pain and hurt to be over and I knew that if he didn't kill me that day he would keep trying. It did not matter that I had a protective order against him. He still would come over. It did not matter how many times I called the police. He would still come over. He would get arrested and then they would let him out. We would have to go to court and he would call and tell me I better not show up. Nevertheless, he did not kill me that day.

That year in Smyrna, GA there were several domestic violence cases in the metropolitan area. Women were getting killed by their ex-boyfriends and current boyfriends. Every time the news came on you would see that another woman that had been a victim of domestic violence. Later that week, after the gun incident, he called me to see if I had watched the afternoon news. I told him that I hadn't watched the news. His response to me was, "Something that almost happened to you earlier in the week just happened to another woman." He said, "I keep telling you to be careful because one day someone is going to find you stinking somewhere in a ditch." It wasn't the first time that he tried to scare me and I knew it would not be the last, but I was tired of going through this drama. This time when I prayed to God I asked that He deliver me out this abuse. I could not handle it anymore and it was not healthy for my daughters to continuing being in that environment. The fall of 2005 was the last time that he ever laid his hands on me. He would still call now and then to make his little smart comments, but it did not bother me as much as it normally would. I was delivered.

The year 2006 came and I began working on self, trying to gain back control over my life. It was not easy. I had a hard time letting people in and trusting people. Sometimes my heart just felt like stone. It was like you couldn't get in and I was not coming out. I began praying asking God to remove the pain and hurt that I had in my heart, but it seemed like it was not going anywhere. I could not understand why things were not moving as rapidly as I would like. Everything was going well with the girls. There wasn't any arguing or fighting in the house. We were a family again, but it just seemed like I could not move any further in my life. So I began to seek God and ask Him why it felt like my life was not moving. He spoke back to me and told me, "You are still holding on to the pain and hurt that you asked me to remove from your heart. How can I move in your life if you are not willing to forgive the person that hurt you?" In my mind forgiveness was hard when you feel that you have done nothing wrong. I was not ready to forgive him for what he did to me, so life went on.

It was spring break weekend in 2007 and we were on our way to Maryland for the week. My chest started to hurt with sharp pains on my side. I drove all the way to Maryland and then back to Georgia in pain. When I got back to Georgia I called my doctor to make an appointment. I went to the doctor on Friday where the doctor scheduled me to have an EKG test, blood work and x-rays of my chest and lungs. The EKG test came back normal, but my chest was still hurting. Before I left the doctor had scheduled me to go see the hematologist because my blood level was not where it should be. I was in an enormous amount of pain. The doctor directed me to rest over the weekend, which I did. Monday came and my chest was still hurting. I did not understand what was going on with me. I started talking to God seeking Him for answers. He simply told me that it was time for me to forgive. I picked up the phone and called the man that had abused and harassed me for five years and told him that I forgave him for everything. My chest stopped hurting instantly. When I went to the hematologist on Tuesday, the test results for my blood were normal. By that Friday my other doctor had called and told me that my x-rays came back and everything looked good. She asked if I were still in any pain; I said no. She could not believe it.

See, all that time I thought that it was my lupus that was causing the issues in my body, but God was ready to start moving in my life. For Him to move in my life I had to start trusting Him. With trusting Him I had to let go and let Him be God.

When you let go and let God be God, things start to happen in your life that you wouldn't believe could happen. I am grateful to God for sparing my life to be able to share my testimony with other woman that may be going through what I went through. If you are going through what I have been through let me tell you that your breakdown will turn into a breakthrough and your bondage will be broken. Through prayer, fellowshipping with women of God and reading my bible my life has changed. I am not the same person that I was and God has given me and my children a new life. My lupus is currently in remission. Start about a fresh start. He gave me a fresh start and for that I am so grateful. Now, all you have to do is trust Him then let go and let GOD. He will always answer your prayer.

Survivor

Teresa Wilson

It was Monday August 19, 1971 and I made my entrance into this world. It was as humble a beginning as anyone else's. I was born to a 19 year old single mother who already had a 1 year old; my sister. It would appear that I had an uphill battle already. My father was present at the time and he was 22 years old with a 2 year old son of his own. So, here you have two young adults with three children between the two of them and no clue of what the next step in life would be.

Life for me was difficult growing up because my mother struggled financially to take care of both my sister and I. To make matters worse, she did not get any help from either of our fathers. I later learned that when my mother took my father to court for child support, my father denied paternity. This incident proved to have negative impact on my life. Nevertheless, my life went forward. I was quiet and painfully shy as a child. I can recall a time where I would never want to speak, for fear of drawing uncomfortable attention to myself. I remember early on that I would always try to "blend in" like a wallflower. I would think to myself, "If I don't say anything people will not bother me." This technique turned out to be a blessing and a curse, because after a while no one expected me to say anything so I was often overlooked, even when I did have something to say!

In an effort to etch out a better future for my sister and I, my mother decided to transfer jobs from Roanoke, VA to Arlington, VA. The only issue was that she would have to leave my sister and I in Roanoke long enough to get herself settled and then she would send for us. This left me baffled, as a child because the one person who knew me the best was leaving me. Logically and financially my mother had made the best and only move possible, but I was crushed. We were in the care of a legal guardian who took great care of us, but she wasn't my mother. I began to think "she left because I didn't tell her I wanted her to stay; I didn't open my mouth." I spent most my life without much to say!

My life continued that way for the next year, with our caretaker caring for me and my sister. We went to church every week because my caretaker had a regular routine. I began to find comfort in our routine, but I missed my mother beyond what I could describe to anyone. I promised myself that once we were back together I would talk to her and tell her how much I loved her and needed her to always be in my life. As the year ended my mother finally came to get us! I can remember not being able to sleep because I knew "mommy was on her way to get us." My mother finally arrived but she was not alone. She had some man in the car with her. It turns out, he was my stepfather! You can imagine my response; silence.

The reunion felt like a betrayal to me. I would often ask myself, "Who was this man, why wouldn't he let me and my sister have our mom back?" My stepfather did try to make us feel comfortable and my sister soon warmed up to him but I, on the other hand, remained as quiet as a church mouse.

Our family was living in a two-bedroom apartment and eventually I was able to reason that this man at the very least would make sure nothing bad happened to any of us. Having a man in the house was foreign to me because my own father had virtually disappeared early on in my life. I could not even remember what he looked like and now I was hundreds of miles away from him so he couldn't find me even if he wanted to. This was the excuse that I comforted myself with. I can remember many adult discussions about money or lack thereof and it bothered and disrupted my family a great deal. I was afraid that my mother would have to leave again to "get more money for us" because after all that's why she left the first time. So I began to try to "fix" things, always making up the sleeper sofa that my sister and I slept on, always removing my plate from the table and never asking for anything. That was my contribution to our family's "money problems." It appeared that no matter how hard I tried the arguments never stopped so I lived in a constant state of fear that my mother would be leaving at any moment.

School was not much of a relief for me. I was away from my mother and could not look out for her so I was easily distracted and always quiet. That behavior landed me in special education classes where I was labeled with a learning disorder. This made me so angry! Children who do not talk are not dumb! And that's what I felt like. While talking was the last thing on my mind, my sister was in special education for the exact opposite reason. She couldn't keep her mouth closed, at least not long enough to learn anything, so she too had a "learning disability." Didn't these people know that these difficulties we were having in school could make my mother "go away again?" So you can believe I got on with the business of "fixing" the problems. The diagnoses for both my sister and I came in the first grade. We were in the same grade because my sister lacked the social maturity to advance from the first grade so we were in the same grade and the same class. By the fourth grade I was reading above grade level and I was out spelling nearly everyone in my class. Even math was a breeze! Whew, I had fixed another problem and assured myself that my mother was not going anywhere.

It was during this time that my mother announced that she was pregnant! I panicked, "we need more money." I began to wonder why she would do such a thing! There was no way I could fix that. My mother gave birth to a bouncing baby boy in January 1978. By this time I had worked out a way to "fix" this problem as well. I would baby-sit so mommy could work and bring more money home. I would also give my little brother all of my food and I would continue with my other remedies. It seemed as if nothing I did worked out. I was scared and hopeless, but determined to do whatever it would take to keep my mom close. My stepfather and my mom went to work every day so I felt that eventually we would stop having so many money problems and the arguments would stop as soon as one of them made more money. Imagine my shock when my mother announced another pregnancy! What in the world was she thinking? September 1979 brought another bouncing baby boy. We were so cramped in that two bedroom apartment. My parents had a room, the boys shared a room and my sister and I shared a bed in the living room. I felt it was better to be in tight quarters with my mother close than to risk her having to go away again.

I remember the moment that I found out we were poor. It was Christmas of 1979, and my parents had to get donated gifts from the local shelter for us. From that moment, I vowed that once I had my own family I would never be poor. There is too much risk for family bad luck if you are poor. My observation was that people who were poor did not appear to be happy. We were always on edge, I was always trying to fix things, my mother was always crying, my sister was always in trouble and my stepfather was always fussing. My life went on this way for many years. This was a "lost" time for me.

Once my sister and I were in high school, my world changed drastically. I remained the wallflower and my sister bloomed into a social butterfly. This was a time that I wanted to be heard because I was tired of people looking right through me as if I didn't exist! To combat my feelings of low self-worth, I buried myself in my books. I did not have the luxury of being comfortable in my own skin. There was an extreme need to be the consummate perfectionist. I made sure that I was on the honor roll each quarter, I worked, and I was involved in after school activates. During this time, my parents ensured that we were all in church. I did not feel a connection in church; I always felt like we were forced to go to church. To me, it was just an extension of our week. I later learned the building (the sanctuary) did not mean as much as having a personal relationship with the Lord.

High school was absolutely torturous because even though I kept myself busy and earned good grades, I was still socially and emotionally stunted. Eventually, in my senior year of high school I met a young man. He attended a neighboring high school, and had no idea that I was a wallflower at my own school. He and I met at a shopping center where all teens congregated and we exchanged phone numbers. We began to talk on the phone and eventually we became a couple. I was 17 years old so this was a big deal for me. This was my first boyfriend and it didn't matter to him that I was quiet, or that I was 5 "10 and 120 pounds, or that I had braces and horrible acne. One can only imagine how I fell for this guy, so much so I ended up moving in with him! Do you see the transition? I went from wallflower to live in girlfriend. I went from going zero miles an hour to 100 miles an hour full speed. Of course my parents did not want this to happen, but what could they do? I was an adult and thought I could do a better job of raising myself anyway.

That fairytale was short-lived once I was no longer a new toy. I quickly learned how disposable I was in this relationship. There were young women that my boyfriend was dating who wanted to beat me up. I would get the frequent hang up calls at our apartment. Not to mention that my boyfriend would simply flaunt the other women in my face! I felt like such a fool. I had given myself to this man. He was supposed to be "the one" so how could this happen to someone like me? I had always followed the rules and had been so cautious. I was so far removed from anything Christian or Christ-like so I did not know what to do next. "If you don't learn from your mistakes you are doomed to repeat them.' I remember reading that quote and that is all I could take away from this painful, pitiful, and degrading situation. I told myself not to worry, because remember

I am the perfectionist. I am the "fixer." Well guess how I fixed this? I remained in the apartment, living under conditions that I would not wish on my worst enemy, while continually taking layer and layer away from my self-worth. Then I joined the Navy! And I left for boot camp after I graduated from high school. That fixed it. In all reality, my boyfriend could have cared less.

The Navy was a great fit for me. I was a regimented, rule following person so and I thought that I had all of my problems solved at that point. The first job which the Navy calls your "rating" I was assigned was less than desirable. I was isolated a lot which was not fun. After successfully petitioning the Navy to change my rating, I was reassigned to the rating of Hospital Corpsman. This was perfect. I was able to help people, and I could get on with my business of "fixing." If it was my job to help and fix and to nurture how could anyone hold that against me and even more important, how could I ever fix myself? I was much too busy now with my new job. There was no time to find out anything about myself.

While I was receiving all of this wonderful training, I began to flourish socially. I was able to talk to people with ease because I sure wasn't talking about myself or what I thought was wrong with me. I met two young men during this time. I went out on a date with the first young man and he was nice and attractive. I couldn't believe that he wanted to go out with me. After the date this gentleman (notice how he now becomes a gentleman!) told me that he could not continue to date me. He said that he knew I was a good person, with a good heart and that he wasn't looking to settle down and that we could be friends. I was 21 years old he was 24. It would take me years to recognize that gesture. I did not like rejection and quickly remembered why I kept my mouth shut for so many years. If people don't know how you are feeling they can't hurt you. "If you don't learn from your mistakes you are doomed to repeat them."

The second young man was the polar opposite to the first, and this date went differently from the first. We went to the local mall and did some shopping. He purchased a cute pink leather skirt in a size that did not fit me. When I asked him about it, he explained the skirt was for his twin sister. That should have been the time that I opened my mouth to let him know there was no way I believed him. I didn't want to be rejected because he was cute so silent I remained. Later that evening after the mall, we ended up at a hotel and sleeping together. Quite a stretch for the wallflower. Hear I was again, from zero to one hundred! Are you noticing a trend?

Almost a year from the time we slept together on our first date, we were engaged. It was the next natural step. We were young and in love or should I say lust. I can remember my mother protesting "but you are only 23 years old!" But now I felt I was grown and knew better. This guy was in the Navy, he had dreams, goals, ambitions, he was nice enough and he was interested in ME. It's a shame that those were my only wants.

It was during the engagement that both my mother and soon to be mother-in-law began to ask about children, religion and a career. Both of them wanted to know what the two of us were thinking. During the premarital counseling I began to get "cold feet." I technically did not have a church home and I didn't have a relationship with the Lord. Also, I still didn't know who I was and I still didn't have a voice. I slept with this guy on our first date! I found out six months into the engagement that my fiancé was cheating on me with one of my closest friends. My fiancé gave me the excuse that, "I just had to prove to you that she really wasn't your friend, she has a bad reputation and I don't want you hanging around her." At this point, I should have opened my mouth, but I did not and by now everyone was helping to plan for this wedding. I just simply could not let everyone know that I couldn't keep a man. From this incident he learned that he could just about do anything and get away with it. My fiancé then convinced me with one week left until the wedding that he needed to borrow sixty dollars from me to get to his bachelor's party. He claimed that this was his last chance to "get everything out of his system." I obliged and he went to this party and two days before I walked down the aisle I found discovered that my sixty dollars paid for the hotel room for my fiancé and his fling! Again if I had accepted Christ in my life or even if I had loved myself just a little more I would have never gotten married, at least not to this guy. My story gets better so please excuse the sarcasm.

I did get married and it was a roller coaster ride to say the least. I received a phone call from my husband's mistress before my first year anniversary. She had called to let me know she was pregnant with my husband's child! Instead of running or even standing up for myself, I got pregnant! That didn't stop my husband though. During my pregnancy, my stepfather passed away. I was surprised at how much his death affected me. He was at that point the closet positive male influence in my life. During this time, I also managed to advance myself professionally. The pregnancy was difficult physically so I remained on bed rest almost the entire time. When I went into labor with my son, I was alone. It was 12:30 am and my husband was nowhere to be found. This was normal at this point. He showed up 2 ½ hours after I paged him, causing me and my newborn son to have to stay in the hospital an extra day to get intravenous antibiotics. Oh, it gets better! This is the point where my husband no longer hid his affairs or unhappiness. He never filed or asked for a divorce. Ironically, neither did I. So as our life went on, I was completely enamored with our son. My whole world centered on him. I began going to school because I wanted a better situation for him, and I wanted to create a better environment for him. I felt like I was the only one in the marriage that cared about our child. Nearly two years later, I found out that I was pregnant again. My husband's response to this pregnancy was to introduce me to his girlfriend. At that point, I grabbled with having this child. Nevertheless, I had my daughter and am so happy I did.

Things went on like this for way too long. I drew inspiration from my children, but I also hid behind them. In other words the children should have been the reason that I left my emotionally damaging situation but instead I convinced myself that I needed to stay with this man so my children could have a   "family." I understand now that they do and always will have a family and their dad will always be their dad. I began to keep myself preoccupied with the children and my career. I was good at that. I progressed through the ranks in the military and my children were well taken care of and loved beyond words. I still didn't know myself and never gave myself enough credit.

I was chosen to attend college full-time while being sponsored by the Navy. My job was to go to school full-time to earn my Bachelor's degree in Nursing while the Navy continued to pay me. This was a huge deal because I was living off one income. While I was working and taking care of the kids, my husband was busy romancing female friends and embezzling thousands of dollars from the Navy. Our personal and professional lives were in complete opposite directions. My husband was found guilty of embezzlement and served 6 months in a military jail. Do you think I left at that opportunity? No! Instead I continued to look the other way as the mistresses went to visit him. Once he was released I thought surely life would change, but it did not!

My husband was so irresponsible at this point that he and I developed a co-dependent relationship. He needed me and I guess I needed him to need me. We were experts at going through the motions.

I graduated, going to school full-time, raising two children, remaining on the Dean's list the entire time I was in school. I also managed to minor in Psychology during this time and graduated as my Nursing class president. I could go on and on about my achievements but this was part of my "mask." While I was busy making everything look picture perfect, my husband floated through life, working jobs that he was obviously unqualified for, because he was fired more times than I can remember.

We purchased a new single family home after I graduated. The picture always had to be perfect and the children appeared happy. Unemployment by then was my husband's profession. It seemed the harder I worked the less he did. I worked 12 to 14 hours a day because of the war. I took care of injured Marines back from the

War front. Strangely enough it was during this time that I started to feel like a hypocrite. I was taking care of young men and women happy to be alive even though they were blown to bits with injuries that I had never seen or prepared to care for. Professionally I had to grow up fast. I would listen and feel the pain that these young people would go through day in and day out and still be happy to just be alive. I felt so dead inside. Why was I so unhappy? I didn't have half of the challenges that these young people had. I began to do some introspection quickly! When did, I didn't like what I came up with. I was miserable, and sick and tired of being sick and tired.

I came home April 7, 2006 and looked my husband in the face and said "What would it take to end this and be fair to you?" He was puzzled and replied, "What?" I replied, "I am finished, let's sell the house and split the proceeds, I want the kid….." I didn't get the rest of my sentence out because I had a fist in my mouth! He hit me! I tried to run, I made it as far as the garage and the commotion caused the kids to start crying and I screamed for my son to call 911. That only made matters worse because my husband was offended that I got the kids involved. He sat the kids down and calmly explained to them that we had a bad argument and that everything was going to be fine. He then directed the kids to go to the family room and play a few video games so we could finish our "discussion." Once he calmed them down he suggested that I go to our bedroom so we could talk calmly without upsetting the kids even further.

I walked to the room and heard the door close behind me, and then I heard the door lock. What was he up to now? To my horror, he pulled a knife out of his sock! I thought he was going to kill me. I couldn't scream because I thought if my kids come anywhere near this madman, he will kill them too. He then made me undress myself while holding a knife at my throat. He put a sock in my mouth and tied my hands behind my back with a pair of my stockings and then proceeded to rape me. I have not ever come to terms with that. My husband raped me with my children in the next room. I was numb. I couldn't think, or feel. Once he was finished, he got up and got dressed, made me clean myself up destroying any evidence of a rape, and left the house.

What happened next will continue to shock you. I took out a restraining order, changed the locks on the door, and filed for divorce. My restraining order was thrown out of court because my husband went and filed a restraining order on me. The Judge listening to both of our cases and then said he could not tell who was being truthful or not so he threw both cases out. I did file charges with the police, but it was two days after the rape. My husband had a warrant out for his arrest and got arrested, but released on his own recognizance. One would think by now that I would have developed a relationship with the Lord. Well, I didn't and tried to fight the legal system on my own. I tried by myself to fight the man who had manipulated and mistreated me for years. Understand that when I say by myself I mean without the Lord.

It appeared as though the odds were stacked against me. The State's attorney told me truthfully that it would be difficult at best to prove rape in a marriage. I was a mess, physically, emotionally, spiritually, and financially. The straw that broke the proverbial camel's back was when the lawyer that I hired for my divorce explained to me that my working hours may restrict me from getting custody of my children. If that was not the irony of all ironies, because I worked hard and my husband was unemployed, I may lose custody of my children. So, I did what I do best, I gave up. I angered everyone close to me, my friends and family had a tremendous amount of emotion invested. People that I loved could no longer stand to be near me because I decided to invoke my spousal privilege and not testify against my husband, the rapist. I felt like I couldn't win the battle, but I would die without my kids.

It turns out that my husband was as happy as he could possibly be. He was spared a possible life sentence for raping me and I continued my life sentence! I had no one to talk to. It never dawned on me to talk to the Lord. I was even more miserable and I didn't think that was possible. I was really going through the motions now. I worked harder, slept more, and ate more. Anything I could do to distract myself. This went on as my husband continued to be unemployed but still managed to stay out all night, only coming home in enough time for me to get to work. He would get the kids up and drop them off at school, lie in bed all day, pick the kids up from daycare and wait for me to get home so he could leave again. This was our life, a vicious cycle.

Then on February 2nd 2007 my husband called me at work and wanted to know what happened to us.

He told me that he hated our lives, and wanted a divorce. I had to contain my happiness because if he knew that's also what I really wanted, then I knew I would not get it. "Are you there?" he asked, "Did you hear me? I want a divorce and my attorney has already drawn up the paperwork, it will be here for you to sign when you get home." He continued by telling me that he would not sue me if I continued to pay the mortgage. At this point I can tell you I lost the small ounce of religion that I thought I had. My response to him was, "You can have a divorce but you got me all messed up if you think I am going to agree to or sign anything that you and your crooked attorney drafted up!" In my heart I knew that I was facing death by going home that evening, but the truth was I was already dead!

When I pulled up at home that evening, I had one of my best friends on my cell phone. As I was on the phone with her, I explained to her that she had to stay on the phone, "It's going down tonight, and he may kill me, but I have to get this over with." He entered the garage and the kids had gotten out of my car and went inside the house to begin their weekend ritual of seeing how late they could manage to stay awake. Once he saw me on the phone he became even more outraged. I recognized his fury, it was the same look of rage he had as he was raping me. He demanded to know who was on the phone, and when I didn't respond he got even angrier. I was still in my car with my windows all the way up and all of my doors locked with a witness on the phone. I foolishly had a false sense of security. Then as quickly as I could blink he opened my car door with his copy of the key and punched me in my face. I thought my teeth were all going to be in my lap, I screamed to my friend "call 911 he just punched me!" My husband then snatched my phone and proceeded to calmly explain that he never touched me. "If you don't learn from your mistakes you are doomed to repeat them."

The police arrived but did not take an official report. The police officer stated, "I can't tell if an assault has taken place, there are no obvious injuries." I had worn a mask for so long the police could not even see my pain literally or figuratively. My husband taunted me and laughed at me. Then he got the kids and hopped into his car and drove off leaving me sitting in my locked car alone with a swollen face, crying. I followed him until I realized that I didn't have a phone and I could really be killed if I continued following him. I pulled off the road and went back to work. A co-worker encouraged me to go to the emergency room as it was visible that I had been hit in the face. I went to the emergency room and prepared to see the doctor. Then my boss walked in. Obviously my co-worker had called her while I was in the emergency room. My boss was nurturing and encouraging and sat with me for hours as I went through my exam and x-rays. Then the doctor delivered the diagnosis. "Your nose is broke," he told me. I don't know of anyone who would be as relieved as I was to have a broken nose but I now had the evidence that I needed against my husband. After my diagnosis, I checked myself into a hotel room for the weekend close to my house so if my children needed me I wasn't far. I then drove myself to the Commissioner's office to file another restraining order because I had proof now. I was going to do it the right way this time. I would soon find out that while I was in the hospital getting examined and x-rayed my husband had went to the commissioner's office to file a restraining order against me.

I then replaced my cell phone and made a call to let my girlfriend and her husband know that I was alive and safe. I then asked her to get me connected with this dynamic aunt of hers who could get me legal help quickly. I talked to her aunt, Dawn Harvey, on the phone briefly, to explain what was going on. The restraining order that I filed was to be heard in court that Monday, as was the restraining order that was filed against me.

On Sunday February 4, 2007 Dawn Harvey entered my hotel room and hugged me and said, "I know everything and it is going to be okay." She then prayed and talked with me and she brought me a bible and her book which was her own testimony. For the first time in my life, I did not feel alone. She then encouraged me to do in my heart what I knew was right, "Give it all over to God" and from that moment on, that is what I did and continue to do.

I prayed all day Sunday, not knowing what to say, or what to pray for. Dawn Harvey directed me to "Psalms 27 and 91" for help and protection, and that was exactly what I needed.

I went into court that Monday February 5th 2007 and the Judge saw right through my husband's charade and granted me a temporary order of protection. She also ordered him to leave the family home and not to go near me the kids, their school or their day care!

We both obtained legal counsel both agreed to stay away from each other and share custody of the kids, alternating weeks with the kids; dropping them off and picking them up at day care. On top of all this, he still had to face assault charges for breaking my nose! Meanwhile I had to keep myself safe, continue to pray and embrace my greatness! I became a new woman, a transparent woman, sharing my story with whoever would listen. How different this was for me!

During the week of February 25, 2007 my husband had the kids and was furious that I would not answer my cell phone. He showed up at my apartment with the kids and banged on my door. I called 911 and took snapshots of him going into my locked car with his spare key. The police showed up and made him go away and my children saw all of this. I immediately went and filed another restraining order. The hearing was on March 5th, 2007 and after hearing both sides, the Judge granted my Order of Protection. Do you see how fast God moved for me?

The assault trial was next. This took place on April 24th 2007. I had my boss, a good friend, my father, and my emergency room report with me. I was surrounded by positive people. The defense attorney successfully negotiated for a continuance. I continue to stay prayerful and surround myself with positive people and reconnect with relationships that I severed because of my relationship with my husband. I enjoyed learning about who I was and what I am made of. With the help of Dawn Harvey, I embarked along with several other women a journey that would teach us to embrace our greatness.

I am now living and enjoying life with my children and reconnecting with lost relationships, both physical and spiritual. The trial date quickly approached on June 19th, 2007. The State's attorney offered my husband a plea agreement that he refused, so the trial began. It was an all day event. I have to say that I was exhausted at the day's end. The Judge proceeded to deliver his verdict: GUILTY!

"No weapon formed against me shall prosper" quickly became my theme. I am now free. Free from abuse from both my husband and myself. I love who I am and who I have become but more importantly, I love the Lord. If nothing else is gained from reading my story, let it be this: Love the Lord, trust in him and believe that "God doesn't make any mess and He doesn't make any mistakes." I have learned to "Embrace My Greatness!"

Love

Me

Kindra Owens

This story is my testimony from loneliness to Godliness. I was born and raised in Long Island, New York, with my younger sister and brother. My parents had their ups and downs throughout their marriage, as any marriage does. I had to watch verbal and physical abuse take place from both of my parents and each time, I would encourage my mother to just leave. "Let's pack up our things and just go," I would tell her. It pained me to see her cry, but she would never leave my father. She loved him. I loved both of my parents but I did not understand their love-hate relationship.

There is one particular incident in my life that I can remember so clearly, like it just happened yesterday. I was nine years old and my mother tried to commit suicide. She thought that her marriage was falling apart and she could no longer deal with it. Witnessing that incident as a young child was very traumatizing. As I got older, my relationship with my mother was strained. I thought that she loved my father more than she loved her children. Instead of wanting to be alive and live for her children, she wanted to take her life because my father didn't want her anymore. It seemed as though she allowed him to walk all over her and treat her like she was nothing and yet she loved him more than her three children. When she came home from the hospital after her suicide attempt, she was never the same. She turned to drugs regularly. I determined in my mind that I was never going to live that way. I vowed that I would never let a man hurt me like that. I would hurt them first.

My parents divorced when I was 13 years old. I had many issues with their divorce that I did not realize until much later. The divorce left a void in my life. I missed my father a lot. He was no longer around as much as I needed for him to be. Eventually, my grandmother took over the role of raising us. I loved my grandmother more than life itself. Even though we lived with both my grandparents and I had three uncles that loved me, it never made up for my father not being there. We always had a house full of people because both of my grandmothers had eight children. No matter which grandparent's house we went to, there was always family so we were always surrounded by love. For me there was just something missing. The absence of my mother and father and the void it left me followed me into adulthood. Several incidents and situations took place that I didn't realize until later, stemmed from my childhood hurts and issues.

As a tomboy growing up, I wore baggy clothes that hid my body because I developed early. I had a woman's shape that none of my friends had and it made me feel out of place, so I hid behind my clothes. When I entered junior high school things started to change. Boys and make-up became the topic of my conversations with my friends. I was allowed to date when I started junior high school but I never really got all dolled up with make-up or worried about getting my hair done. I was plain looking. This was largely because of a comment that my grandfather made to me one afternoon. I was getting ready to go out and I decided that since all of my friends were wearing makeup, I was going to put on some makeup too. I was using the mirror in my grandparent's room to get ready and my grandfather walked by the room and saw me. He said, "I don't know why you are in the mirror, you are always going to be ugly." That statement devastated me. "Why did he have to say that to me?" I thought. "Was I really ugly?" I rationalized that he was simply mad about something and decided to take it out on me that day. I continued to get ready and left. That statement hit me hard and made me suspicious of guys that told me I was pretty. My own grandfather said that I was ugly so they must have been lying to me. My parents' divorce, my view of my mother and the comment that my grandfather made hindered the way that I was able to interact in my relationships and how I responded to men. I wasn't necessarily looking for someone to be a father figure to me but I fell into the habit of always wanting to have a man around, but only on my terms. I needed to have their attention, whether good or bad.

By the age of 16 I thought that I had joined the ranks of women. I gave away the only treasure I had that was supposed to be a special part of me. Afterwards, I still felt like a little girl. It wasn't the way I thought it would to be. When I entered high school, I was so lost and in need of unconditional love that I was determined to have a baby. I believed that having a child that would love me unconditionally would resolve what was wrong with me. So, I became engaged when I was 18 to a basketball player at my high school. My fiancé had no problem with my look. Actually, he loved it! I often wondered about his true feelings for me. Why did he like me? Did he really care about me or was he just getting what he wanted from me? He did think that I was pretty, but I didn't believe him. We tried unsuccessfully for two years to have a child. In my mind, I believed that having a child would fill that void in my life. I didn't understand back then that God had a plan for my life and that's why I was never able to conceive. Eventually, I became depressed because I honestly thought I was not able to have children. I thank God that He does not always give us what we think we want when we ask for it.

I could not wait to graduate from high school. I wanted so badly to get out of New York and away from the life I was living. After graduation, I moved to Maryland to attend college at Morgan State University. I was so eager to get a fresh start. See, then, I still did not know what was wrong in my life, but one thing that was for sure was that this new life in Maryland was going to fix it! I moved in with my aunt who was only six years older than me so we clicked right away and were close. We enjoyed doing the same things and had fun together. Even though we were close it never occurred to me to sit down and talk to her about the things that I was feeling and going through. I started school that next semester, made some new friends, and I got a job. It finally seemed as though everything was beginning to look up, until the day that I went to the doctor. I hadn't been feeling well so I decided to be proactive and schedule an appointment. That was the day that I learned that I was pregnant. I was in complete shock at the news of my pregnancy. I had already made up in my mind that I could not have children after my previous failed attempts. On the ride home from the doctor I went through several different emotions. I was shocked, then scared, then happy and overwhelmed. You will never believe what happened when I arrived back home. When I got home I had to immediately call my aunt and have her come rush me to the hospital. Much to my horror, on the same day that I found out I was pregnant I also had a miscarriage.

Even though I was emotionally devastated by this experience, I allowed myself to jump right into a new relationship. I don't even think I gave myself time to heal from the previous relationship and the devastation that was attached to it. On my 21st birthday I found out that I was pregnant again. I was so excited and nervous at the same time. I prayed for a happy, healthy, beautiful baby that did not look like me. I gave birth to a beautiful baby boy that looked just like me. A year and a half later, I gave birth to beautiful baby girl. My prayers for her were the same; that she be healthy, beautiful and not look like me. Until I had my daughter

I still dressed like a tomboy. This changed when I received an invitation to my friends wedding. I had to wear a dress which was something that hated to do. That day was different. I looked in the mirror and was pleasantly surprised by what I saw. While at the wedding, I received attention that I was not used to receiving. I liked the attention that I was getting because in a way, it made me feel like a woman. After the wedding, I went shopping and invested in some formfitting clothes. At the time, I thought it was a great investment. I was getting a whole lot of attention with this new look. This look was going to be my new weapon of warfare with men. See, I had already made several attempts at having meaningful relationships being the way I was, but it didn't work so I decided that I was going to live a little. I was going to worry about me and me alone.

This begins the turning point in my life where I started down a path that I never thought I would recover from. I was looking for the idea of love that I had seen so many times on television. In my opinion, love meant that a man was supposed to sweep me off my feet and tell me he loves me and take care of me for the rest of my life. He would look deeply into my eyes and I would be able to see that he loved me without him saying a word. The only place that a man looked deeply into my eyes and whispered sweet nothings to me was in the bedroom. Therefore, I began to equate love with sex and figured that to feel loved, I had to have sex. So, my thought pattern was that I would not let a man walk all over me, but knew that to feel loved, I had to have sex. I didn't want any relationships because time had already proved that relationships don't last. I always managed to get hurt. I can have the sex without the relationship and get everything that I need, or so I thought. I played out this thought process in my life for about three years. I had gotten to the point that I was so burned out and used up that I had to make a change. The positive part about this time in my life was that God gave me the sense to not allow my behavior to be seen by my children.

At the age of twenty five I was again given the opportunity for a fresh start. I decided to join the military. I was away from my children and my family for about five months so I had a lot of time to think. I made the decision that when I got home, I had to change. First and most importantly, I was going to be a better mother to my children. Then, I was going to settle down and get married. I vowed to date a different type of man.

See, the caliber of man that I was used to dating was not working out in my favor, so it was time for something new. What I didn't realize then was that I was picking and choosing my mate instead of letting God select who He wanted me to be with.

My grandmother had always told me that I should date a man that likes me, not a man that I liked because a man that liked me, would take care of me. I thought her reason was crazy nevertheless, I decided to give it a try. I was so happy to be home, and anxious to start a better life for me and my children. I wanted them to be proud of me and the changes I was making. Things started out well. I threw out all my old phone numbers and stayed away from familiar places that I had once visited. I was happy about this new change. The next relationship that I entered had the same outcome as all the rest. I know believe that was because I still wasn't allowing God to fix the root of the problem, which was me. I was running from relationship to relationship, never stopping long enough to allow the Lord to work on my behalf. Looking back, I now realize that I was a very needy girlfriend. I had to be around my boyfriend all the time. It wasn't that I didn't trust him; I just didn't want to be alone. If he was not able to give me the time and attention that I needed then I always had someone on reserve that was able to meet that need. So, I fell right back into my old pattern of getting what I wanted and moving on.

By 2004, I was in such a depression that I was regularly calling out of work, not answering the phone, and not leaving my house. If I did go to work, I would sit in my office and do nothing. In the evenings at home, I would put on my happy face for my children of course, but just until they were in bed and asleep at night. When I was alone, I felt as if I were dying on the inside. I cried myself to sleep many nights because I had no one to talk to. I could not figure out what was wrong with me. I kept that routine up for about a month. One afternoon I was at soccer practice with my kids and started talking with another soccer mom. She asked me if I knew the Lord. My response to her was "If I accept God, then I have to accept the devil and I don't want to deal with him." She then started asking me about Halloween and if I knew the real meaning behind it. At that time I didn't, so at the next practice she gave me a brochure to read and to do my own research on the topic. When I saw her at the next practice she invited my children and I back to her apartment because she had forgotten another brochure she wanted me to have. The kids went into the backroom to play and she and I sat down and started talking about the Lord. The one question that she asked me was, "Are you saved?" My response was "I don't think so." I said the sinners' prayer and gave my life to the Lord right there in her living room. That evening things changed for me in ways that I could not even begin to explain. I, myself, didn't even know what was happening. The following Sunday I decided to visit her church.

Now, I must say that I did not grow up in church. My grandparents went every Sunday and were active in their church. My parents were forced to go to church when they were children, so they chose not to go as adults. After I had my children, there was a strong desire for me to attend church. What I didn't know was the Lord had been calling me for some time. I had prayed and asked for things with the promise that I would go to church. I never held up my end of the bargain when God came through for me. The last time that I asked for money and He sent it, I told Him that I would stop playing and go, which I did. I found a couple of churches in my area and went. They all appeared to be the same. They were small, musty, and confined places with hard, uncomfortable pews. They choir sang songs that I did not know and the people shouted and fell to the floor, and then they asked for money. I went to about five of them before I stopped looking. I just gave up and told myself that church was not the place for me. I did not want to be around those people because I thought they were all pretending. When I finally agreed to go to church with the soccer mom, my mind automatically went back to those days but, I had promised God that I was going to stop running, so I went.

As I pulled into the parking lot of this church, I was impressed with what I saw. The building was beautiful. My first thought was, "Not bad." I drove around the parking lot and found the soccer mom's car and parked next to her. She had forewarned me to get there a little early to get decent parking. I watched the people that were walking through the parking lot. They all appeared to be so happy and eager to get inside the building. That was one thing that I had never witnessed while visiting the other churches. Finally, I made my way out of my car and followed the crowd that was entering through the back door. When I entered the building, I was again impressed. The church had a day care. I took note of that, just in case I decided to visit again with my kids. I had never stopped walking when I entered the door, so I was still following the people as they made their way up the stairs. When I made it to the top of the stairway and walked into the foyer, I was sold. I expected to smell old cedar and stale air. That was not the case. When I walked into the foyer a greeter walked over to me and gave me a friendly embrace. Now, I was not used to that at all. I jumped back in shock at first before realizing what her intentions were. She told me to go into the sanctuary and to sit anywhere that I wanted to. I followed her instructions and as I made my way toward the sanctuary doors they were slowly opened by an usher who offered more hugs and escorted me to my seat. I was so nervous because I didn't know anybody and didn't want to appear as though I did not belong there. It was obvious that I was a visitor.

As I settled into my seat, I finally got the opportunity to look around the room. Even though people were walking around and talking, the atmosphere was so quiet and peaceful. Soon after, the praise team began to sing. They really sounded good. Okay, so I was in my element by then. I was enjoying myself. I felt like I was apart of what was going on. The pastor was up next. They called him the "Man of God." As that man of God spoke to the congregation, the Holy Spirit was speaking to me. I had no problem following along with his message because he didn't shout, growl, or scream at me, as I had witnessed so many other preachers do in the past. As I left, I realized that I had really enjoyed myself. "I think I'll come back next week," I thought. That is the only church that I have been to more than once and it is now the place that I call home.

During my first year at my new church home, I learned a lot of about God and about myself. My Pastor was teaching heavily about staying away from sin and why it was so important. All my life I had heard people say that you were not supposed to have sex until marriage. I just thought it was an old fashioned view about life. I never knew that it was in the Bible. Because I was growing and learning, the enemy came to trip me up. You see, he could not allow me to become too strong in my faith and in my walk with Christ. Satan's first attempt to sabotage me failed miserably. I give God all the glory for this. His next attempt at destroying me began when men from my past began to call me, wanting to get together and "talk." I was able to abstain for a while, but eventually I fell. I knew that it was wrong and yet it felt so right that I laid aside my common sense and faith in God for my feelings and emotions.

I struggled for two years to break free from the bondage of sexual sin that I had walked right back into. I continually looked up and read scriptures dealing with fornication over and over. Two scriptures that God lead me to read were 1 Corinthians 6:13 and 1 Corinthians 6:18-20. 1 Corinthians 6:13 told me "…Now the body is not for fornication, but for the Lord…" and 1Corinthians 6:18-20 further stressed to "Flee fornication, every sin that a man doeth is without the body; but he that committeth fornication sinneth against his own body. Know ye not that your body is the temple of the Holy Ghost which is in you, which ye have of God, ye are not your own? For ye are bought with a price; therefore glorify God in your body, and in your spirit, which are Gods."

When I first read those scriptures I did not fully understand their true meaning. Now I know that I belong to God in every aspect of my life. Jesus died and gave himself as an offering for my sin so I could have the opportunity go to Heaven after accepting Him as my Lord and Savior. While here on earth I am supposed to glorify God with everything that I do. When I was in high school and my friends and I would hear the word celibacy, we would laugh and call the other girls prude because they weren't fooling around. Now I realize how silly we were. Celibacy is neither a funny nor a dirty word; it is what God calls us to be as single men and woman.

The word of God teaches us how we should act as husband and wife. It also teaches us the things that are acceptable to do when we are single. The world has made it acceptable for men and women to have multiple sex partners therefore accepting fornication as the norm. The word of God tells us that we are supposed to remain pure until we get married, then become one with our mate that He has chosen for us. Celibacy is a cleansing and purification process. It is a time for you to get to know yourself again and to get back into relationship with God. It also allows you to learn what He says about you. Once you allow yourself that alone time with God, you will come to the understanding that no man is worth separating from Him. If you allow Him, He will provide you everything that you need and will give you the desires of your heart. If it your true desire to be married then allow God to choose your mate for you. A man should learn to love God first and foremost and once he has accomplished that, then there is nothing that he would do to defile a woman or his vow to God. Once I finally got that revelation in my spirit I was able to break the soul ties I had with the men I had allowed in my life. I was able to get back into my studies and spending time with God. I believe that I lost all of that because of the guilt that I felt about the relationships I was in. I wasn't going to church regularly and I wasn't praying like I should have been. I allowed those situations to steal my fire for the Lord. No longer is this the case.

I was looking for love through having sex instead of addressing the real issues I had, which stemmed from my childhood. My grandfather telling me that I was ugly and my mother being on drugs, her attempted suicide and my fathers' absence in my life were major issues that I chose not to address. By listening to my Pastor teach, and reading the bible, I was able to see exactly where I was and how I got there. The first thing that I had to do was forgive my mother. I carried around hatred for her because I thought that she loved a man more than her children. I always felt that she was weak-minded for her decision to attempt suicide. What this did to me was make me weak. My wanting to be in control of everything made me vulnerable without evening knowing it. Talking to my mother about this was one of the hardest things that I've ever had to do. Our relationship had always been shaky at best. We would talk only when we needed to or on holidays. Now, I had to call her and have a conversation. It turned out to be the best thing for both of us. She explained to me a lot about my childhood that I didn't know about. We talked for almost two hours and when we finished we were both crying uncontrollably. Today, we are closer and now in the healing process. My conversation with my mother also helped me to understand that my father leaving was because of the issues that they had and not because of me. I was able to put that issue to rest and begin to heal in that area as well.

Along this journey and in my prayer time, I came to the realization that in all those relationships I was searching for the approval that I thought I never received from my father or grandfather. My father always loved me but was not always around because of circumstances that had nothing to do with me. As a teenage girl learning about boys and sex, it would have been paramount for him to have been in my life, as an example for me to follow. My grandfather loved me but was just not an easy man to deal with. He was always going to say what was on his mind no matter what. My grandmother prayed for me all the time and it is because of her prayers the Lord kept me. As I look back over the situations that I have gotten myself into, I know and understand that it was only God that kept me. I had been in situations where I could have been physically abused and even killed. I thank God that He didn't allow me to marry the first man that said he loved me. I would not have been happy, just married. I could have contracted incurable diseases from any one of those men but God's grace and mercy kept me. He kept me long before I knew anything about His goodness or how much He loved me.

Since regaining the inner strength that I have so many times given away, I have felt such a load lifted from me. I am able to sleep comfortably and my conscious is clear. Being able to sit and listen to God and act on what He says is the best thing in the world. It still amazes me how God knows when and where to send the people that will move you to the next level in your walk. I met my life coach through a business venture. We were at an airport coming home from a conference and both of our flights happened to be delayed. We ended up flying home on the same flight. We were not able to sit together but when we got off the plane she said to me "God told me I am supposed to help you. I don't know what it is, but I am to make myself available to you. If you need me for anything, please call me." She then told me about a personal development class she would be teaching later in the year. I knew that I had to take that class. It was well past time for me to get serious about seeking God. Taking this class with other women who are seeking God and learning who God says that we are is so empowering. Having someone to talk to that understands what you are going through and where you are trying to get to is so fundamental when you are growing in God. We are all like-minded women with a common goal. It's liberating to watch, encourage and help one another attain what we need for our personal lives.

Now that I am back on solid ground, I am able to state with a voice of triumph that I have been celibate for a year and half now. I am happier than I have ever been. That period of my life is complete and I trust solely in God to sustain me. My only hope it that my writing this will be able to help another person come through their situation victoriously. I would like to thank Pastor Dawn M. Harvey for this opportunity to nurture and help someone else to grow, and to the women of Embrace Your Greatness. Thank you for your love and support.

I'm

Free

To Be

Me

Mary Christine Grice

After the death of my father, I experienced abandonment. As I began to heal from these feelings of abandonment, terrible things began to happen to me. I suffered years of abuse and molestation. This left me confused throughout my life. I never realized the molestation I went through would have such an impact on my life. As I grew up, I began to block it out of my mind. It wasn't until I was delivered and set free from past hurts and pain that I able to confront these issues. Even though I had given my life to Jesus Christ years ago, I was still lost until I committed to a sincere relationship with Him. The word of God says the truth shall make you free. I feel in my spirit that it is time for me to share my personal testimony.

At the age of eight I lost my father to lung cancer. This is where my feeling of abandonment initially began. I felt abandoned because at the time of my fathers' death, I had little understanding of the meaning of death. I was so unaware and uneducated about death and dying that at my father's funeral, I can remember sitting in my older brother's lap posing and smiling for the camera while everyone mourned. My father had been sick for a while before passing away. We had many good times together. When he would come home from work I would be waiting to greet him. My siblings and I made up songs for him and would stand outside singing until he drove up to our house. After he came inside, he would sit down and relax in his favorite chair. I would take a comb, a little black comb that I received from school whenever I took pictures, and sit in his lap and play in his hair. My fathers' hair was so soft and curly that the comb would glide right through. I would repeatedly comb his hair until he fell asleep. As the days went by, the cancer eventually spread causing my father to spend more time in the hospital than he did at home. I was so busy playing and staying away from home that I was oblivious to what was going on with my father.

The day finally came when my father passed away. We were all at the hospital when it happened. Because my siblings and I were so young, the hospital would not allow us to be in the hospital room, so we had to sit in the waiting area. I can remember when my family came downstairs and announced my father's death. The realization of death finally set in. I was so hurt and angry. I had nothing but mere feelings of rage and resentment on the inside. They didn't even let me say good-bye! At the time, I hated the hospital for this.

That was my father and I was never going to see him again and they still kept me and my brothers from going upstairs to see him. Didn't they know that he wasn't coming home to us anymore? This was what I was feeling on the inside. Now, I can say that despite everything that happened, God is good.

As I reflect, I can hear the Lord saying "I heard your cry and it's not too late to say good-bye." God didn't directly speak those words to me, but He showed me exactly what He meant by allowing me to have a second chance with my father in a dream. My mother kept a chair in her room for my father when he was sick so he could sit up and relax. I was asleep in her room one night after my father's death. I woke up sometime during the night and saw my father sitting in that very chair. We called my father by his last name, so I called out Grice! I ran to him and sat in his lap like old times. I began to tell him how I felt about him and that I love him. God only gave us a brief moment together but that moment seemed like a lifetime. It was like a breath of fresh air. After telling me that he had to go, we both said good-bye, and instantly he was gone. I got into bed and went back to sleep smiling inside and out. From that moment on, I felt peace. I was no longer angry with the hospital. I was able to move on. I was able to finally accept his death.

God has a way of bringing healing to a person no matter what age. At such a young age He gave me a dream that took away lasting pain. God is a perfect God. His power is real. He is a loving, gentle God and a God of order. I pray that as I write this, those of you who have experienced the loss of a love one will begin to understand who God is and that He is capable of healing you through your pain. I can feel his presence as I am writing. My prayer for you is that healing will began to take place in your heart, mind and soul.

Not long after my father's death, I began to experience abuse through molestation. The abuse began when I was eight years old. I was a normal child. I did the normal things that an eight-year-old would. I was also timid and shy. I cannot pinpoint the exact moment the molestation started but I had many sleepless nights. There was a pattern in how it took place. When I would go to sleep, my abuser would come into my room and take advantage of me. I eventually told myself I was never going to fall asleep so he wouldn't touch me. It was hard trying to stay awake. I would be so tired that all I wanted to do was sleep. I thought that if I sat up on the couch all night watching television, then I was safe. Of course, I would drift off to sleep only to wake up fighting him off me. Well, the time came when I couldn't fight sleep anymore so the abuse continued.

As the years past, he got bolder and it didn't matter if I was asleep or not. He would threaten me by saying that if I told anyone I was going to be in big trouble. He said that if my mother found out she was going to beat me to death. It got to the point where I was tortured by being made to say things that I didn't want to say. If I was stubborn by not responding to him, it would get worse. So, I would just go with the commands I was given. I felt trapped. I would avoid coming home in the afternoons by going to a neighbor's house. I figured that by not coming home, I would be able to escape the abuse. I guess I wasn't smart enough because he would just come find me and say it was time for me to come home. Now, I knew my mother wasn't home. I would always tell my neighbor, "I don't want to go." My abuser would tell my neighbor that my mother said I better come home now. What could I say then? So I went home and sure enough, when I got home no one would be there. It was just him and I alone. I tried to cry and whine and say, "You lied; I knew my mother wasn't here!" Crying didn't work because after he told me he was sorry for lying, he took advantage of me.

There came a time during this ordeal where I thought I couldn't take anymore. I was tired of him controlling me and running my life. It got so bad that he didn't even want me to have male friends. I just wanted the nightmare to be over. I wished it would just stop. I began to want bad things to happen to him so he could pay for what he was doing to me. I believe it was at this point that God stepped in allowed me a way of escape. I moved from North Carolina to New York. Whenever I came back to North Carolina he would still hurt me. Then, he moved away. As I got older I got a little bolder and wiser. When I turned fifteen, I was able to handle him. He would come back to visit, thinking I was still that little girl that he could take advantage of, but I would boldly tell him "NO."

I remember a time when he came home to visit and tried to take advantage of me. By this time, I had moved back to North Carolina. He decided to pick me and my friends up from school one afternoon. As he drove us home, he tried to make a move on me while driving. After living in New York for that short period of time, I wasn't the same fearful, timid little girl he was used to. Normally, I would have kept quiet but at that moment I swung and screamed at him. He was so embarrassed and shocked that all he could do is pretend like he didn't know what was going on. Everyone in the car was completely quiet. In a fit of rage, I boldly declared to him, "You know what you just tried to do. I am not going to take this from you anymore." From that day on, it was over. I was finally free! I never had to worry about him molesting me again. My friends never questioned me about the incident and I never offered any explanations to what took place in the car that day. I praise God because that was the last time he ever touched me. At last I thought, the years of abuse and molestation were over. No one was going to ever touch me again.

As time went by, I began to wonder what happens after the molestation ends? At first you're just relieved that it's over. Is it ever truly over? Have I forgiven myself and my abuser? Have I allowed healing to take place? Am I pretending that it never happened by blocking it out of my head? Just because the molestation was over, doesn't mean that it didn't impact my life. What began to happen was that twenty years later it left me confused. I harbored the spirit of not forgiving others on the inside. All those years following the incident, I now realize that I wasn't truthful with myself. I was running from situations all my life, by not wanting to face them. I trained myself not to remember my past. In essence, I was in denial. I would watch talk shows about women that had been molested and think to myself, I was molested and it never bothered me so why can't they get over it? I thought that being molested never affected me. But it did have a major affect on my life. I was in wrong relationships. I loved everyone but myself. There were times in different relationships that I settled out of fear because my mate wouldn't take no for an answer. My friends didn't understand why I stayed in the relationship as long as I did. Anytime I felt threatened in a situation, I would give in. Therefore, this caused me to begin to hate the other person.

Another way my life was affected was that I allowed everyone to have control over me. I never knew who I was and what I wanted in life because I did what everyone else wanted me to do. I felt alone. To those of you who have people in your life who don't understand why you're still talking about things that have happened to you; please understand that they don't understand what they haven't been through themselves. Some of the things that people would say were, "Let it go, it happened twenty years ago, and why are you in that abusive relationship? You need to leave him." Even though these individuals were close to me and it hurt me when they minimized my pain, I kept pressing my way to the only one who understands. You too have to find someone who understands. God will always understand what you are going through. Tell Him all about your troubles. Just when I thought no one was listening, He heard my cry. No one knows what it's like to be in your situation unless they have faced it themselves. I am not telling you to continue to dwell in the past or to stay in an abusive relationship. You've got to let go of every negative situation to move forward and you don't have to go through it alone. Cry out to Jesus and He will see you through.

Another aspect of this is we must to learn to love ourselves and find out what makes us happy in life. You see, I never knew how to love myself. Forgiveness was a start for me because I was waiting for God to punish the people who hurt me, so I could be happy. I wanted to ask Him, "God how can this person walk around happy after what he has done to me?" I want him to pay dearly for hurting me. I now understand that it wasn't my prayer for that person to suffer that would set me free. It was when I began to believe God and forgive myself and others that I began to heal. I was missing out on life by carrying around what a person did to me. It wasn't worth it.

I now refuse to let my past keep me captive. A person's mistakes are not worth the benefits that God has for me. No one is worth my soul. Those are two principles that I try to live by in life whenever I face circumstances. Four years ago, I forgave my abuser, my older brother for hurting me all those years. And since then, I have taken my life back! To God be the glory.

One day one of my sisters stated that she noticed how I was never in any family portraits. I began to tell her all the things my brother had done to me and how I hated him. Then I began to tell my other sisters. I told them how I never forgot about what he had done to me. I didn't want to be around him that's why I was never home for family functions. I would go to New York just to get away from him. One of my sisters began to tell me how sorry she was and that she never knew I felt that way. Later, I began to come forward with other siblings. I struggled with the intimate details. I wanted to be subtle for the sake of my family, but I asked the Holy

Spirit to move because someone needs to be set free and delivered and by my story. I pray that this will be a door for Christ to dwell in you so healing can begin to take place. If there are any abusers reading this book, I pray that you will ask for forgiveness, confess what you have done and forgive yourself. I pray that the victims will not harbor unforgiveness but seek forgiveness for you and your abuser. I also pray that you will cry out to Jesus and tell Him all about your troubles. If He can do it for me, He can do it for you.

It wasn't until God sent a childhood friend back into my life that I began to recognize that I hadn't been delivered from the molestation. She became a mentor and life coach to me. I joined her personal development program "Embrace Your Greatness." As I began to learn about myself old wounds began to open. I then realized that I had never dealt with the pain, I only blocked it out of my mind. Through reading Joyce Meyers book "Beauty for Ashes," I have learned to trust and depend on Him and His promising word. It's been about five months since I began to recognize why I was the way that I was and why I stayed in abusive relationships so long. I thank God for my weaknesses because through my weakness He is made strong. For all the women that I have judged for being in situations, forgive me as I forgive myself for being in denial. I've been born-again for several years now and there are still shattering strongholds in my life, but I am able to recognize my strongholds and identify them. I realize the abuse played a major part in my character. But the same God who showed up when I was eight is still showing up at 38.

Through Christ Jesus I am more than a conqueror. I'm not saying that I don't face trials, I just conquer them knowing that I have a peace of mind and that I have a resting place in Jesus. Therefore, I can do all things through Christ which strengthens me! Through His son Jesus Christ, whom He sent for the remissions of our sins, and the Holy Spirit whom is our comforter, I am now made whole! Jesus can do the same for you if you seek Him. He tells us to knock the doors will be open to you. That's why it is important that I share my testimony with others who may not have the same strength, and courage to be set free.

I was at a church meeting one evening and even though I was afraid, spoke up and I mentioned that I was a victim of abuse. Well, after the meeting a young woman met with me outside and thanked me. She was glad that I came forward because she too had been abused. She wanted to speak up but she was afraid. You see, every time that I would hear that still small voice speak to me, I would miss it and regret it later. Well this time I followed the voice and was glad I did. Again, that's why it's important that I share my story.

To my mother, I love you unconditionally. I pray that you understand that I had to be set free. To my biological sisters, I pray the sharing of my testimony will set you free as well. Thanks for loving me and helping me in all that I do. To my brother, in my heart I forgive you. I used to express happiness when you would face situations in your relationships, but now I'm asking you to forgive me as I have forgiven you. My prayer for you is that you will go to God and ask Him to forgive you as well. My prayer for you is that you make it right before God.

Finally, my ultimate prayer is that for anyone who reads this chapter, you be eternally blessed by what you read. With the help of God and Pastor Dawn Harvey, I have been able to pour out some of the most intimate details of my heart and soul. Be encouraged knowing that God is in control. God Bless.

Can He

Cover

My

Anointing?

Lillian Perkins

Dealing with being single for the past four years has been a bittersweet experience. I never would have imagined in a million years that I would be a single mother raising four children. Although the start of my single life was challenging, God has given me the grace to handle it. My faith and belief in God is what has kept me through the rough moments. Staying grounded in the word of God has given me the courage to continue to press through each day. 2 Corinthians 12:9 says that "My grace (favor and loving-kindness and mercy) is enough for you (sufficient against any danger and enables you to bear the trouble manfully); for my strength and power are made perfect (fulfilled and completed) and show themselves most effective in (your) weakness." When I think back to the day I realized my marriage was over, I can still recall the pain, hurt, embarrassment, confusion, betrayal, anger, resentment, and the fear that I felt.

Staying in an unhealthy marriage was trying. I was mentally drained, but fighting to stay married because of my children. My husband would tell me everything was fine, but his lack of support and attention proved otherwise. I was constantly looking at myself in the mirror doing a self-check on what I could change about myself, all the while, chipping away at my self-esteem. What could I change about myself to make him to love me the way he once did? I was weak in my spirit and feeling dejected. I knew I needed to replace those thoughts and feelings with the Word of God.

There was a time when we were very happy. We had two children at the time and we both enjoyed our jobs. We had just bought our first home and he asked me to have another baby. At first, I disagreed, but when I did agree, I became pregnant instantly. About four months into my pregnancy, my husband fell asleep behind the wheel and hit an 18-wheeler, while driving home from work. When I opened the door and saw the police officer, I got an uneasy feeling in my stomach. He asked if I were Mrs. Perkins and told me that my husband was being rushed to the area hospital. I immediately rushed to the hospital and got there before the ambulance.

Once he arrived, and I was allowed to see him, the first thing he said to me was "where is my mama?" My response was, "WHAT?" That stung for a minute. The enemy was busy all ready. For a split second, I felt hurt and betrayed, but I rationalized that he was medicated and this was not about me right now. Back in the waiting area the doctor came out and told us that he had two broken ankles, a crushed knee, a broken jaw, cracked chin, and a broken hip. He was banged up pretty bad. The doctor also told us that he would not walk again for at least a year. The doctor continued to tell us that because my husband was dressed in his uniform at the time of the accident, the breastplate in the bulletproof vest he was wearing saved his life. My initial thought was, "I hear you doc, but I know who really saved his life."

My mother stayed at my house for the next couple of weeks with my kids so I could stay with him at the hospital day and night. I seemed to be running on overdrive. Two days before leaving the hospital, I was able to wheel him over to my first ultrasound. It was then that I found out I was carrying twins. My first reaction was complete shock. I immediately looked at my husband and stated, "Don't you tell anyone!" He said, "Not even my mother?" I said, "NOBODY!"

At a time that I should have been so exciting, I was overwhelmed. I was truly numb about being pregnant with twins. I did not talk the rest of that day or the next day. I knew I would love my twins very much, but at the time, I wasn't sure if it was the right time. Although I was in shock, my husband very was excited. I had to go to God to let Him know I was feeling overwhelmed and I needed Him so much to help me stay encouraged. God did promise that He would never leave me or forsake me and that He would perfect everything I'm concerned about. The Lord led me to read Psalms 138:8 which say "The Lord will perfect that which concerns me: thy mercy, O Lord, endureth forever: (forsake not the works of thine own hands)" I meditated on this scripture often.

In the mist of my husband's accident and the shock of the twins, God truly showed up in our life. The events of his accident were in the local newspapers all over the area. Fellow officers donated sick time, the local railroad donated money, and the police department gave a crawfish boil and a golf tournament in his honor. People we didn't know donated money and that continued for a while. All I could say was "look at God." The true blessing was that he was up and walking again in six months instead of twelve months. That was right on time because my doctor put me on bed rest the same week he was cleared to be able to drive again. I thank

God that He worked our situation out so we never had any lack or need during this trying time.

After the birth of our twins, I wasn't sure what my real role was anymore. I knew we would spend time with our kids bonding as a big family, but as soon as he was released to go back to work, he was gone. This was two weeks after the birth of our twins. So, after an emergency cesarean, and months of bed rest, I was stuck at home with four children. Where was the support I needed? I didn't know anything about raising twins or four kids for that matter. So, I did what I knew best. I turned to God. The word of God told me in Philippians 4:13 (AMP) " I have strength for all things in Christ Who empowers me; I am ready for anything and equal to anything through Him Who infuses inner strength into me: I am self-sufficient in Christ's sufficiency." God would equip me with whatever I needed so again I had to stand on the Word.

At one point, I tried to go back to work, but that didn't work out. I ended up a staying at home. I wore so many different hats, that I began to feel unfulfilled. I decided that after my twins were a little older, that I would go back to school. I knew that raising four children, having a husband and home and going back to school was going to be a challenge. Once again, I knew that my Father promised me that I could do all things through Christ, who strengthened me. I discussed my desires with my husband and he appeared to be supportive. He told me he would help me study. The first day I had to study, he sat with me briefly and for the next two years, I received no support. Each day I prayed over myself, my family and what I desired. Then I began thanking God for it in advance.

When I graduated, family and friends joined us at a local restaurant to celebrate. For my graduation gift, he bought me the car I had been confessing as mine for months, a Lincoln LS fully loaded, sunroof, wood-grain, black exterior, and nice rims. I was so excited. That night, while family and friends showed me love and support he was distant and didn't talk much. At dinner, he barely spoke to anyone. I tried to play it off by asking if he felt well, but no response. I attempted to thank him, but still no real excitement or expression of support or happiness. Once again, I didn't understand why he was not happy for me.

We often talked about moving to Dallas. Since graduating with a degree in Computer Information, I set my eyes on working for Microsoft. I was expecting to get the job of my dreams. I wanted it so much that it didn't matter what position in the company I started with. I believed that any position would be my foot in the door for great things to come.

A couple of weeks after graduation, I applied with Microsoft in Irving, Texas. I know the Word say ask, believe and receive. When I asked the Lord about working for Microsoft I believed at that moment that I would get hired and nothing or no one would be able to stop me. I was determined. It was settled in my heart and I was expecting God to give me exactly what I had asked and believed for.

As I drove to Dallas alone for my interview, it dawned on me that each time he went on an interview or took a police officer exam, I was right there with him to support him. Why, on my big day was I on this journey alone? Maybe this was time I needed to reflect on things and talk to God and actually listen to Him. At the time I began to feel a shift in my relationship with my husband and I couldn't explain it. I had to encourage myself and allow my thoughts to stay positive.

As I approached Microsoft, I was both excited and nervous. I was on a mission and I needed more than ever to believe that I would walk out with my new position. After my first interview there was a second interview, which was unexpected. At the end of my second interview, I they thanked me for coming and told that they would make their decision in the next two weeks. I was excited but didn't want to get ahead of myself. On my drive home, I continued to thank God periodically, if for nothing else, just for the experience. When I got home, a representative from Microsoft was calling me. When I heard her voice, I wasn't sure what to think, but she proceeded to tell me, "They love you and want to know if you can start in two weeks." Look at God! I hadn't been home 30 minutes. I reminded them of my situation and that I lived 4-5 hrs away. She told me that if I needed more time to let her know, but she really wanted me to start training in two weeks. Thank you Lord! My husband ran into the room to see what I was screaming about and when I told him Microsoft offered me a position, he looked at me and said, "That's good." My first reaction was, "what's wrong, I thought this is what we have been praying about" and he said, "It is, nothing is wrong, I'm happy for you." And he left the room. I did not understand it, but I knew in my heart that something wasn't right. I was too excited about how fast

God moved on my behalf and I began to thank and praise Him.

The plan was that he would keep the kids at home with him, with the help of his mother and our baby-sitter, and I would go through training and stay with our friends in Dallas, while looking for a house. Meanwhile, he was still contacting different law enforcement agencies as well as police stations in the surrounding Dallas area. I had reservations about the arrangement, and wrestled with staying and giving up my dream job or going and trusting God that things would work out.

I made the decision; I took the job. For the first week it appeared that all was well. As I toured Microsoft and realized how well Bill Gates provides for his employees, all I could do is thank God. In the first week, I found a house that would be great for us. My husband received a call from a police department in the area as well. One night, during my second week in Dallas, I was saying good night to my kids, as usual, and I asked to speak to my husband. As my daughter hesitated, I asked her what was wrong. She told me that he was at work. It was 9pm! I could not believe he left our children home alone. I felt helpless. I told my daughter to call him and tell him that I had called and I wanted to speak with him. I asked the Lord to place a hedge of protection around my kids. I prayed that ministering angels would keep them safe from any harm or danger.

When he called I was calm. When he told me that he left the kids alone to go to work, I went off!! We never used profanity with each other, but I had a way with words that could grip him better than using any profanity. He began telling me that he didn't want to move to Dallas and he was only doing it because of me. He went into details about Dallas being my dream not his and how he didn't want to work at the police station where he was recently offered a job. I could not believe what I was hearing. You live with a person for so long and you think you are growing and moving in the same direction and to find out in this manner was simply crazy. I pleaded with him to go home to be with the kids and he refused. He told me I could come home or stay if the job was that important to me. I was amazed at how he was trying to manipulate and control the situation. He knew how important family was to me.

Once we hung up, I called my kids back and I talked to them until they were sleepy. I prayed with them, said good night, and cried myself to sleep. The next day, I went to work and explained that I had a family emergency and I had to go back home. She understood and told me that my position was secure and if I needed to go, just keep her updated. After driving two hours it began to thunderstorm. I blasted my praise and worship music cried and prayed. It felt like my life was falling apart. My prayer to the Lord was "please allow me to get through this storm and home to my kids and I will never leave them again." I didn't realize that I was about to go through a real storm in my life in the natural and in the spiritual realm. Going through challenges, we tend to get stuck in it, never realizing that if we keep pressing through or walk that thing out, that we will come out on the other end. Usually we come out better than we could ever have imagined. Don't get stuck in the midst of the storm, and stay, because sadness or depression will show up. Know that someone else has been through a similar situation so you are not the first person to be experiencing it right now.

We go through challenges and trials in life and right in the middle of it, we want to slow down, stop, cave in or quit, but if you just keep in mind that it will end at some point. Just don't quit! The Word tells us that in this life we will have tribulations. However, "It came to pass." As you look into the rearview mirror of your past, you realized that you are still standing. God brought you out of all of it and He deserves the glory.

Once I arrived home and had a chance to talk to my husband in person, I began to wonder, "What was really going on?" I could not wrap my mind around the fact that this man was married to me, a woman of God, who supported him in everything. My only desire was to take our family to the next level but he couldn't see that. He told me that I could go and he would keep the kids with him until I got settled, if Microsoft was that important to me. He even stated that eventually he might come, just not now. It seemed to be some type of ultimatum. I wondered what else he had pretended or lied about. The real question was "Can he cover my anointing?"

The decision was hard; I cried for 2 days. I was so messed up on the inside that I couldn't hear anything God was trying to tell me. I contacted an attorney about my situation. She told me to stay because if I left my kids with him, he could say that I abandoned my family and a court would give him the kids if there was a custody battle. This was not what I wanted to hear. It simply was not fair. Why was I being penalized for having a dream of bigger and better for my family?

When I made the call to Microsoft to explain that I had to resign, surprisingly, she told me that she would hold my position for three months. I was so excited thinking this would give us time to work things out or time for me to come up with a plan. Once the three months had come and he still did not want to move, I resigned from my position at Microsoft. I believe at that point, resentment showed up. Months past and I could see us growing apart; he was spending more time at work and I was alone a lot with the kids. I started feeling rejected and dejected until my self-esteem was not where it used to be. I could feel myself changing and going into a state of loneliness. I was going to the movies alone, trying to convince myself it was because I enjoyed my own company. I was married but still felt alone. I withdrew socially from everyone. I could not explain it. Our conversations became only about the kids, the house, or the bills. It was getting bad. The real storm had arrived and I was in the middle of it. I yearned for a supportive-loving relationship. The breaking point was in 2002 when the kids and I went to visit him at his off duty job and he wasn't there. When I called and he finally arrived, he was upset. I didn't want to believe that he could be doing something behind my back, but in my gut I knew. When the kids and I left, my daughter made a statement that would change my life and force me to confront the truth. She said, "Mommy, does Daddy have a sweetheart. My response was, "Yes, I'm his sweetheart." She stated, "No Mommy, another sweetheart beside you?" For my daughter to say that to me, I thought she either knew something or the Holy Spirit was revealing things to me through her. Either way, I needed to know what was going on.

I can't describe what I felt but this put me on a mission from September 2002 to October 2002. For that month, it was hard to keep a straight face and to act as if nothing were wrong. I had to put on the game face so no one would know that I was going through my own "hell." I remember many nights waiting for my kids to go to sleep, and going to my garage and sitting inside my truck to cry; so long and so hard that at times it was hard to breathe. I remember times of lying on the floor of my daughter's bedroom in the fetal position crying so much because it hurt so badly. The next day, I would be smiling with my kids and trying to reassure them that everything was going to be fine. They were hurting just as bad. I felt hopeless, helpless, rejected, alone, and ashamed. It was as if on the inside I was like shell broken into a thousand pieces but on the outside the shell was intact, beautiful, like no damage was done.

Not only did I believe that I wanted the generational curses to stop, but I had to search my inner self and realize what I am worth to God. I am an uncompromisingly righteous-bold woman of God, a child of the King. I am fearfully and wonderfully made and no weapon formed against me shall prosper. God has a plan for my life, plans of good and not evil- to give me a future. God said all these things about ME! I knew that I needed to trust Him.

On October 14, 2002, we drove to Houston to our church. That day our pastor was talking about husbands being the "man of honor." The men at church were selling hats with "*Man of Honor*" on them, and he asked me to buy him a hat. Now on the inside, I was thinking "is he serious? But I bought the hat. On the way home, I had to laugh to keep from crying. I knew I had to follow through with my plans and this day our lives would change. It was the beginning of the end for us. Enough was enough.

That day after he left for work, I took the kids to our childcare giver to stay overnight. Once his shift ended and he went to his usual Sunday night hangout, I put on my tennis shoes, grabbed my camcorder and left the house. The GPS that I had placed inside the car lead me straight to his mistress's house. He had been going to see her every Sunday after work. With my car in the middle of the street, I called inside and said to her, "Can you tell my husband to come outside?" I could see the blinds move and someone look out. In less than a minute, he walked outside. I turned on my camcorder with the spotlight on him and said, "I just needed to see it for myself." He never looked at me and never said a word, but he knew that he was caught. The word of God says that what is done in the dark, shall come to the light.

Four months later, on February 19, 2003, I was officially a divorced single mother of four. Set free from the bondages of an adulterous marriage, and the pain, shame, and hurt that went with it. Now it was about God and me; He had to help me work on healing my kids and myself. The day after our divorce was final he was named "Police Officer of the Year." How funny was it that, I put in all the blood, sweat and tears and someone else got to enjoy the fruit of my labor.

The pain became even more intense because two weeks after my divorce was final, on March 9, 2003, my mother died suddenly. She was only 53. The same week, I was in a major car accident and almost lost my life. The enemy was on a mission to steal, kill, and destroy. I was slipping into depression and I didn't realize it. People close to me started to notice. There were nights when I didn't sleep at all because I was trying to figure out why this was happening to me; what did I do to deserve this happening all at once. I was angry with him for hurting me and the kids. I was angry and feeling guilty because I wasn't there when my mother passed away. How could I get pass this pain that was so intense and so deep.

So after days and months of crying and feeling sorry for myself, I decided I did not want to feel the pain I was going through any longer. Even though I was crying out to God, the pain was not going away fast enough. The Word of God had to work, because I had to get past this. I reminded Him of his Word; that He said He would never leave me or forsake me and that He promised to perfect everything that I was concerned about. My children and I were suffering and we needed God to restore everything the enemy stole and then some. I pressed everyday, asking God to not allow me to be bitter, jealous, or angry. I was determined to hold God to his Word. It was a trying time.

I had to realize that I am a priceless overcoming victorious woman of God and I deserved much more than a man who *could not cover my anointing*. But did I learn right away- no I did not. I wrote God a claim form telling Him what I wanted in a man. Over the course of the next 2-1/2 years, I wondered if I should have stayed with my ex-husband to at least have a piece of man verses no one at all. I had asked for my man of God to be a Boaz. I met all kinds of guys during this time. I knew from the beginning that nothing would transpire, but in a couple of the situations, I wondered could he be "the one."

In every situation in which I allowed them to get to know me, I would hear the very same things. You're so sweet; so classy, intelligent, funny, beautiful, and smart. You're a strong black woman taking care of your business. Nowadays, the real question is who is willing to go to God on my behalf? Who is willing to pray with me and for me? Who is willing to tell God on me- instead of getting upset because I didn't do it his way? Who is filled with the Holy Ghost, speaking in tongues, tithing, and who can handle me being a bold, uncompromisingly righteous woman of God and continue to support me? *Who can carry my anointing?*

God knows what is best for me, and I understand that He is a jealous God and does not want me putting anyone else before Him. I began to see what it is about me that they kept mentioning. It was the anointing on my life. I believe in my heart that I am destined for greatness. Some days I confess it and other days I cry out to the Lord asking Him what is my purpose? What am I supposed to be doing for Him while I am here? I know that I don't need to focus on my Boaz, or on my new house, or my new car, but focus on God.

I decided to consecrate myself and live a life of celibacy. I find that when the issue ever comes up, men want to know "Why?" I want to know "Why not?" It wasn't always easy; there are times when I was tempted. Once I rebuked the enemy and let him know how serious I was, I have not had a problem in that area. I am not tempted in that area because I know the ultimate goal for me is waiting on that my man who God has prepared especially for me, the one, who will find me. I don't look anymore at different men I see or talk to wondering 'is he the one'. Nothing else but a man who is true to God is going to work for me now.

Knowing my purpose is important to me now. Also raising my kids to be intelligent, spiritually strong, well-rounded human beings with goals, dreams, visions and purpose is important to me. I find myself wanting so much for my kids. I want the time to spend being there for them. I have a strong desire to provide for them, to put them through college and to build that big house that we vision and talk about constantly. Ultimately, if I can help one person avoid going through what I went through it will be all worth it. I stand on several scriptures in my walk with Christ. The main one that is engraved in my heart is 2 Corinthians 9:8 (AMP) "And God is able to make all grace (every favor and earthly blessing) come to you in abundance, so you may always and under all circumstances and whatever the need be self-sufficient possessing enough to require no aid or support and furnished in abundance for every good work and charitable donation."

Since I have been putting God first and taking my mind off a relationship, I can see that to be in a healthy relationship, I need to work on me and embrace who I really am. I also need to regain all of my self-confidence and stay focused on God and my kids. I have come to realize that I can no longer give so much of myself so quickly in a relationship. I am learning so much about myself right now and learning that singleness is not bad. It is a gift. I am learning to love myself. No one can steal my peace.

As began to read and listen to material by different pastors and ministers, I have taken away something from several of them that helped to sustain me in my everyday life. I realize that it can help sustain any woman who has been a victim of physical or mental abuse.

Throughout this whole devastating experience I have asked God to purify me from my past so I can see who I really am. I just really want to thank Pastor Dawn Harvey who shared her life story in a way that ministered to my heart. She shared with me how important it is to embrace my greatness and how to expose the enemy and share my story. Then I can heal and began to understand who I really am. She taught me how to go deeper than just surface healing. Pastor Dawn Harvey has showed me how vital it is to open up those past hurts and really expose the enemy. All the secrets and things that I didn't want people to know don't even matter, because what others think about me is none of my business.

I remember sharing with her that I felt as if I had been standing on the end of a cliff waiting on someone to push me so I could grow wings on the way down. I can say that my life has changed in the last several months. I am happier; I laugh more than I have in a longtime. That is a blessing to me. I'm not where I need to be but I thank God I'm not where I used to be. I've known for a while that I am destined for greatness. My life is changing as I embrace my greatness. I challenge you to "Embrace Your Greatness" and walk into your destiny.

"You have been carrying around everything you need for the rest of your life, all of your life"
- Dawn M. Harvey

Purposed

By

Design

Ebony Wood

Coming from where I'm from, the average person would have thought that I would be a seriously messed up person. Some of the experiences that I have had, however small to others, have ultimately shaped and molded me into the individual that I am today. In essence, I am the sum total of everything that I have been through. The past four months of my life have been an experience that has led me to exposing my most intimate life journey, my testimony. My very being has changed since joining the class "Embrace Your Greatness." I am not the person I used to be. The air I breathe is even different. God, through the help of my life coach and many blessed women of God, has showed up in my life like never before. It is because of Embrace Your Greatness that I am able to share my story. I thank God everyday for sending me my life coach. You have been a mentor, friend and spiritual mother to me. You have enabled me to see that God has a special plan for my life. You helped me realize that I am destined for greatness. It is my sole purpose to share these delicate matters of the heart with other young women who may have had similar experiences and can't see the light at the end of the tunnel. There is a light, and it's a light that cannot be hidden.

At the age of six, I had my first experience with death. And it so happened to be my sixteen year old brother. My mother gave birth to him at the tender age of twelve. Some years later, he went to live with his father, who was older than my mother. This was a situation that we had to get used to because we were a family, but it was for the best. Subsequently my mother conceived and gave birth to another boy, then myself, and then my baby brother. None of us had a father in our life. One thing you should understand is that I come from a family of very intelligent individuals, and my oldest brother was no different. He excelled both academically and athletically. He was an all around great kid who played every sport and mastered them all. I was very attached to him. He was so popular and I was proud to be his little sister. I made sure everyone knew that he was my big brother. He was the first hero I ever had. People told us we looked just alike. When we were all together, I was the happiest person in the world. I felt like nothing else mattered. Even though we did not live together, he treated my brothers and I as if we were the most important people in his world.

It was a very hot day at the end of May, and my school had dismissed early. After getting off the bus, my brothers and I went to play outside in the hot sun. We were just so grateful to be out of school the heat and humidity didn't really matter at the time. After playing for a while, our neighbor came outside to find us. She told us that mom had to leave because something had happened to our brother. We returned to playing outside and waited for our mom to come back. When she didn't come back by the evening, I walked to my aunt's apartment to find out what was going on. My aunt who was visibly upset told me not to worry about it; it would all be explained later. That night my mom came home upset, crying and depressed. My brothers and I learned that our hero had died in a swimming accident where he attempted to dive into the water, hit the bottom of the creek headfirst, broke his neck, and drowned.

This tragedy impacted me in a major way. I didn't understand what death was or how someone came to die. What happens when you die? That was the question in my mind. No one really took the time to explain to me what it meant because everyone was too busy grieving and mourning. At the funeral, there must have been at least two hundred people gathered for this home going ceremony. Sitting on the second row next to my brother, we were both quite confused. I remember nudging my brother on that second row pew and telling him that I had to use the bathroom. He told me to hold it, and mom would take me when she stopped crying. We both sat watching and wondering why our beloved brother was taken from us.

To this day, I will never understand why God took an angel away from me. I was torn apart inside. In the years that followed my brother's death, I felt that because he died and didn't stay with me, that's why bad things happen in my life. I was only six and never got the opportunity to let him see me shine the way I did as a child. It was almost like the most important part of me was taken from me and because nobody ever showed me how to deal with my emotions and feelings; I kept them inside a box-my heart.

This is where I began my journey of being a quiet, shy, reserved yet friendly girl began. There is a saying that says "eyes are the windows to a person's soul." I was never one to say much. I didn't really need to because my eyes were able tell you everything you needed to know. Because of this tragedy I believe my mother slumped deeper into depression, drugs, alcohol and the life that accustomed all of those things. I began to take notice to this and because I had no outlet and I didn't know how to grieve, I held all my feelings and emotions within me.

My mother's addictions had a major impact in my childhood. Some of the situations my brothers and I were exposed to were unbelievable. Several times I witnessed my mother being abused physically and sexually by various men. Sometimes the police would come and the man was arrested, only to return in the morning with apologies. There were times I would have to run out of the house in the middle of the night to get help because of a man beating on my mother. I always felt the need, especially at such an early age to protect my mother. I would lie in my bed at night when the fights would take place and cry until I couldn't take it anymore. My brothers would sleep right through it most nights. It was hard for me sleep through yelling, fighting and my mothers pleas for him to just stop. Sometimes I would sneak out my bedroom window and run to my aunt's house. Other times I would run to the second floor to a neighbor's apartment. I always felt relieved and comforted when the men were arrested. The sad part is that they always came back. I could never understand why they were allowed to wreak havoc in our home, however unstable it already was, and then be able to return. This made me feel depressed and dispirited because I felt like it was my responsibility to protect my mom and she didn't see it that way. Although I was dispirited, I never allowed her to see that side because in some odd way, I felt that my feelings would upset her. As much as possible, I tried to keep my feelings and emotions inside so she wouldn't worry about me. If she wasn't strong enough to fight, then I wanted to be strong enough to fight for her.

One evening, shortly after the death of my brother, my mother took me into the bathroom to talk to me. There were people in our apartment and she needed to speak to me in private. She explained that she loved me and that we were just alike. When she looked at me she saw herself and it scared her. She didn't know how to handle me. At the age of six, I didn't understand the magnitude of her words. She explained to me that I was going to go live with my aunt, whom I was very close to. She said that I could still visit but for now, that's where I was going to live. The boys would stay with her for the time being. Later that day, my aunt came to pick me up.

Once again, I didn't understand why this was happening and why my mother was being taken from me. In the months to follow, I was allowed to see my mother whenever I chose, as long as she was in the frame of mind to allow me to see her. During this time period, my grandmother also stepped in and played a major role in my upbringing. Off and on for about a year, I was back and forth between living with my aunt and with my grandmother. There were times where my mother would be so caught up in her lifestyle that I would go weeks without even being able to speak to her. It was like pouring salt on that open scar. This hurt me to my heart, but just like everything else that I didn't understand, I kept it all inside.

I can remember when my mother met her first husband. He was a boxer. They were engaged and married in a very short time. During their engagement, he began to beat and hit on my mother often in front of my brothers and I. There was a time where they got into and argument in the supermarket over a box of cereal that my brothers and I wanted. Well, he didn't want us to have it. He began to raise his voice to us and then threw the box of cereal on the floor. My mother took us out of the store and went to sit in the car to wait for him to finish shopping. He came out the supermarket very hostile and angry. My mom started the car to leave, and as we are pulling off he opens the driver side door and reaches in and wraps his hands around my mom's neck and starts to choke her. By this time, my brothers and I are yelling and crying for him to stop. When he wouldn't stop, I jumped from the moving car and ran across the parking lot to the payphone to call the police. As I was talking to the dispatcher, I remember hearing my mom yelling and say "I'm not marrying you, you don't love me." The police arrived a short time later and arrested him. I was crying uncontrollably because I honestly thought he was going to kill my mother in front of us. It took a lot to calm me down that night and get me to sleep. I did not sleep well that night, thinking he was going to sneak in and kill my mom. In the morning he returned with an apology. A few months later they were married at a big lavishing wedding. Shortly after, they separated and then divorced. Years later, reflecting on this situation, I couldn't understand why God allowed me to experience this. Why did my brothers and I have to go through seeing our mother treated like this? At that age, this experience emotionally devastated me.

A few months after my mom separated from her husband, she and my brothers moved in with my other aunt. They had nowhere else to go then. My mother was still addicted to drugs and alcohol. She would often leave my brothers with my aunt for periods of time. Neither I nor my brothers would hear from her for awhile. One particular time, my mother left for the weekend and didn't return. My brothers remained in the care of my other aunt. Days and weeks went by and we were unable to get in contact with her. One evening, as I was playing in my room, my aunt called me to the phone. The voice I heard on the other end send waves of joy and happiness throughout my entire body. It was my MOM. To hear her voice after so long was the best thing in the world at the time. She apologized to me for not seeing me in so long. Then she explained to me that she was in the hospital getting help for her problems. She said that everything was all right but she would be in the hospital for a while longer, and after she was released she would go straight to a recovery home for drug and alcohol survivors in Baltimore, Md. I asked about my brothers and she assured me that my other aunt was going to take care of them, and I would remain where I was. My brothers took the news rather hard. They were angry, upset and hurt that she would leave us like that.

When she moved into the halfway house, we visited whenever we were allowed. Over the course of about a year she was making progress in the right direction. After being released from the home, my mom was able to get her own apartment and begin to take the necessary steps to get custody of her kids back. We were very happy to be reunited with our mother. I can honestly say that after not living with my mother for almost eight years, the only thing that mattered was that I was home. I was so excited on the inside; I was unsure how to act because things were different. My last memories of living at home were not the best. So, I was a bit apprehensive to say the least. Yet and still, I suppressed these emotions because I wanted to be with my mom.

From the age of six until fourteen while going through all those trying times, I must say I was a very fortunate child. My aunt who I must say raised me well, loved me, supported me, and encouraged me. She instilled biblical values in me. We attended church every Sunday. According to her, there was nothing I could not do if I set my mind to it. She would always tell me how pretty I was, and how intelligent I was. All this was great; the only missing piece to this puzzle was the presence of my mom. I had a hard time accepting this so I never discussed it with anyone. Because I was always complimented and praised for doing well, this caused me to always seek approval from others. I always wanted people to be proud of me. I always wanted to be a people pleaser so I had a hard time saying no to people. I just didn't want anyone to be mad at me for any reason. This trend continued throughout my life.

When I went back to live with my mother at the age of fourteen, I was in desperate need of that mother-daughter bonding. I felt as though I had never had it. Yes, I had my aunt, but she was not who I called mom. My mother did her very best to try to make up for lost time, often giving my brother and I whatever we asked for. She worked two jobs and weekends to support us alone. She began dating a man who was very nice. He treated her well and was nice to us as well. Eventually my mother and this guy got an apartment together. I was uncomfortable with this situation because I wasn't ready to share my mom with another person if I didn't have to. I never expressed this to her though. My mother's intents were on getting married. After some time she found her way to church and gave her life to the Lord and took a vow of celibacy. She began to be active on the usher board and really committed to God.

After walking as a Christian for a period of time, my mother was eager to be married to the man she was dating. After having several conversations with him and realizing that he was not ready to be married or willing to go to church, she knew in her heart it was time to move on. In our apartment, we had three bedrooms. My mother moved all her things into my brother's room, and for about six months, she slept on his bottom bunk bed. Eventually I started sleeping in his room also, because she was in there. The reason I began to sleep in the same room with my mom and brother was because I felt a sense of security with all of us being together like that. I was protecting and standing by my mother's decision of holiness. I felt that I needed to be near her to protect her from herself. I wanted to be close to her wherever she was. We eventually moved out of that place and back into a place of our own. This was a huge step in the right direction for my mom and we supported her every step of the way. I never questioned her motives and decisions about what she was doing. I was there to give her my quiet support.

By this time my mother had been drug and alcohol free for over five years. She was on the right track in life. Part of me kept waiting for her to backslide or slip up and revert, but she did not allow that to happen. I believed that she would leave us again but she never did. She was about her Fathers business and taking care of her kids. We finally had time to focus on just being a family again. It was an overwhelming feeling for me, one that I had never felt before.

As we grew in the Lord as a family, there was a Deacon in the church that my mother took a liking too. He was a nice man who served the Lord. My mother began socially dating this deacon from the church. He seemed nice enough. He seem to genuinely care about us and wasn't out to get anything from us. He would take my brother and I out after church to eat. I remember a time when my mom was between paychecks and low on money and we didn't have much food in the freezer. I suggested she call her friend the deacon. At first, she refused. Well, she did end up calling him and explaining her situation. He told her to meet him in thirty minutes. When we met him he said hi to my brother and I. Then he handed her a fifty dollar bill. As she stood there amazed he quickly hugged her, told her to go take care of whatever she needed, and he would talk to her later and left. Now, in my mind, I was wondering what man would just give a woman with a fifteen and thirteen year old money and not ask anything in return. It just seemed suspicious. I had seen men walk all over my mother, and this seemed like one of those "this for that" situations. Well, it didn't turn out to be one of those situations.

Eventually after another year, they got married. He bought a home for us to live in. He treated us like we were his own kids, providing our every need while treating my mother like the queen and the excellent wife that she was. I was amazed and grateful. I believed that he was just what she wanted and needed. I felt that God was rewarding my mother for all of the trials and tribulations that she endured. It was at that time that I believe my mother finally stopped grieving the death of her firstborn child. I was content in knowing that God was looking out for us.

I had always known I was smart, pretty and special. That was obvious to me. The fact was that because I knew these things, it scared me. In a sense, I was afraid of myself. I wasn't sure who I was going to become. In my freshman year of college, I can remember walking down the dormitory halls one day, headed to my room. As I walked past a group of females I overheard them saying "There goes that girl, she's too quiet, maybe she's gay." I believe that those females intended for me to hear them, but I didn't stop walking, I just kept on to my room. Once inside my room, I sat on my bed and just stared at nothing, wondering, "What is wrong with me? Why would someone think that about me?" Of course, I knew I wasn't gay, sure I liked boys, but I didn't have a boyfriend, nor was I talking to anyone. That situation really took a slice out of my self-esteem. It made me become even more self-conscious of myself. I decided that most people did not have my best interest at heart and because of this I never had more than one or two friends. I didn't realize how special I was in Gods eyes. He had His hands on my life, that was a fact, but a small part of me didn't understand why I had to be so different from everybody else. After my second semester of college, I came home because my parents couldn't afford to send me to such an expensive school. Now, I was devastated. Internally I had died and given up on life. The one thing I wanted to do, I couldn't. I never once blamed my parents, because the truth was, I didn't want them to suffer financially. I don't think they knew how torn I was by not being able to continue school.

At this time in my life, I began to realize that even though I had it together on the outside, I was a basket case on the inside. My thoughts about my life consumed my mind. If you can picture a civil war scene with cannons and guns and a battlefield, then you can understand my mindset at this time in my life. It was like a battlefield. I had issues. I lost all confidence in myself and who I was. I didn't understand why God wouldn't just make everything better. You see, I was beginning to see the confidence that I displayed on the outside was fake and artificial. The real me, the inner me, was filled with confusion, instability, and turbulence. On the outside, I was good, couldn't be better. I began to experience waves of depression, anger, temper problems, negativism, attitude problem and a controlling spirit. What was wrong with me? My spirit was dying. I didn't know what my purpose was in Christ. I knew the word of God but that wasn't enough. I didn't know who I was in God. I knew who I was pretending to be on the outside. There was something missing and I wasn't sure about how to fill that void. I felt that I needed to find myself. I needed a break from everyone and everything. Just going to church wasn't really enough for me. There was more to this Christian walk and I was missing it. I didn't like the feeling of missing the mark with God.

At the age of 19, I joined the National Guard. This wasn't a hard decision for me. I wanted to go to college and the military paid for college. I needed to get away from my surroundings, and the military would do just that too. I would be required to go through about six months of training. It seemed like just the right avenue to take to find out about myself. My family thought this was a good idea also. To them, it was a way for me to come out of my shell, to open up, meet new people, and see the world. Little did they know, I just needed to get away. Now don't mistake me, I knew this was a very serious decision. I thought that by joining the military, I would find myself. This proved to only be partially true. What began to happen was I started to react to life situations and the emotions and feelings that I was having. In case you are confused, I will explain. Previously, I would not confront situations, feelings or emotions. I only let them build up and consume me. Basic training forced me to react to situations, feelings and emotions because the environment was so stressful. God put me in a place where I had not choice but to look to Him for help. It took only a short time to realize that while some things changed, I still had some of the same issues. I was able to conquer my fear of people. But what I realized was that I still longed for something. I wanted a purpose and didn't know where to begin to find it. I needed to know what my destiny was. Exactly what did God put me on this earth to do? You see, the military only taught me character, I needed purpose!

My church family was always very supportive of me. Whatever I needed, they were there. My step-dad who was the assistant pastor always kept them up-to-date on how I was doing. The truth was, I was coming to church Wednesday after Wednesday and Sunday after Sunday but wasn't getting much out of the service. It was all getting to be monotonous to me. The spirit of God was there but it just seemed to be the same scenario every Sunday. I came to the conclusion sometime after my 21st birthday that I was not growing anymore. It was time for me to move on. I remained faithful to the ministry for a while, but I was not focused. I began to share this with my parents so they suggested that I start visiting other churches. They told me they would support me in whatever decision I decided to make. I thank God for my grandmother during this time as well. My grandmother played a part in my decision to move on as well. I can still remember her statement. She told me in the most unpretentious manner, "Well, nobody knows your soul better than you and God." I don't think that she realized the impact of those words or what they meant to me but it was all I needed to hear.

One Sunday while I was at my military unit for drill, my supply sergeant asked me if I would like to go to church with her during lunch. I was a little hesitant but said yes anyway. From the moment I walked into the sanctuary I could feel the Holy Spirit in the room. It took me by surprised because I had not felt the move of God like that in a longtime. As I stood there observing in amazement as the praise team ministered and then the Bishop spoke, I was taken aback. I began to feel warm inside. At that time, I didn't realize that it was the Holy Spirit that was on me. About a month later, I began to visit that same church more often. The more I visited, the more I felt God pulling me toward that ministry. It was just crazy, in a good way. I was learning and felt my spirit coming alive more and more. My parents could see the change in me also. They never said anything though. I believe that they were just sitting back and watching the Lord do a wonderful work in me. For the first time in a longtime, I felt a little stability. I continued to visit this church regularly. Notice I said visit because I had not yet became a member. Part of me still felt a certain loyalty to my church and my pastor. It was home to me. Everything was familiar and I knew I was welcome there. Now, I also knew I was welcome at this new church but everything was different here. I only knew a select few individuals. It was all unfamiliar territory to me but something was pulling me there.

Now, that's not the happy ending to the story. I really wish I could say that after all of this, everything was great. What I had to find out the hard way was that, the enemy is always busy trying to destroy our lives. You see, when I took that first step towards God, the devil was mad. He was caught off guard because he was used to having me right where he wanted me. Scared, confused, afraid to move and paralyzed with fear. So, the enemy regrouped and came back, full force. The bible clearly states in John 10:10 that "the enemy comes *only* to steal, kill, and destroy..." That's his only purpose in our lives. He wants to see us messed up and falling apart because then he knows that his purpose is being fulfilled.

So, as I began my journey into a more fulfilling life as a Christian, as well as a young woman, things began to happen. I was in unhealthy relationships that God didn't ordain for me to be in, I was suffering financially because of disobedience to God, and I began to put God second to many things. I was still growing in the Lord, reading and understanding my bible, and communing with God, but at a much slower pace than I should have been. I didn't know back then that God desires a personal relationship with His children. Just as we have relationships with our family and friends, the Lord desires to have an intimate relationship with each one of us. He needs to be able to communicate with us one-on-one. God wanted to a personal relationship with me so He could talk to me. One of the first things the enemy tried to do was make me think that God wasn't hearing me. I would often question if He was actually listening to me when I talked to Him. It wasn't that I couldn't hear Him; I just doubted what I heard. So really what was happening was the enemy was trying to take my mind. He knew that if he could get my thoughts and emotions, then he had me. There were many times the Lord would speak directly to me and tell me to do something and I would doubt Him. I would be too afraid to do what it was that God was telling me to do. You see, there's that fear creeping back up on me. The devil was busy! I felt like I was right back to square one.

Even though I made some changes, refocused and reshaped my mind, I still wasn't where I needed to be. I wanted to know who I was in God. I wanted to do His will. I began to realize that all that time I was searching and searching, God just wanted me to trust Him. He wanted me to have faith in Him and believe that He had my back. He was right there all the time, just waiting for me to look up and notice Him. He never left me. He just wanted me to stop doubting and start believing, and so that's what I did. I began to trust God like my life depended on it. I joined the class Embrace Your Greatness and since then, my life has never been the same. The most important aspect that we must always remember is that 2 Timothy 1:7 states "God has not given us the spirit of fear but of *power,* love and a *sound mind."* I am not perfect, and I don't always do things the right way. What I know is that God loves me, in spite of all my shortcomings and faults.

There is a poem that hangs on my refrigerator door. I hang it there, because whenever I go into my refrigerator, I can't miss it. This poem reminds me of me. It inspired me and I want it to inspire you also. The title of the poem is *"What is Your Deepest Fear?"* By Marianne Williamson.

*"Our deepest fear is not that we are inadequate.
Our deepest fear is that we are powerful beyond
measure. It is our light, not our darkness that most
frightens us. We ask ourselves, Who am I to be brilliant,
gorgeous, talented, fabulous? Actually, who are you
NOT to be? You are a child of God. Your playing small
does not serve the world. There is nothing enlightening
about shrinking so other people won't feel insecure
around you. We are all meant to shine, as children do.
We were born to make manifest the glory of God that is
within us. It is not just in some of us; it's in everyone.
And as we let our own light shine, we unconsciously give
other people permission to do the. As we are liberated
from our own fear, our presence automatically liberates
others."*

This poem has blessed me. It speaks directly to me and is so simple to read and understand. I am a child of God, a royal priesthood, a holy nation. You are a child of God. We are all meant to manifest the glory of God! He wants to use us all to do a mighty work for the Kingdom. We have no reason to be afraid. Past situations, experiences, people, places should not hold us back from being who God called us to be. He brought us through all types of events. He told us He wouldn't put more on us than we can bear. So if we are going through, it's because the Lord has a perfect plan to bring us through. Romans 8:28-29 states "And we know that in *all* things God works for the good of those who have been called according to His purpose. For those God foreknew he also predestined to be conformed to the likeness of his Son…" We have been predestined. We are destined to prosper. That's how much God loves us. He only wants the best for His children. As I write this, I am ministering to myself. I too had to come to understand and believe that God has a perfect plan for my life. He made me the way I am for a reason. He wants to use all my talents and abilities for His glory. I believe that God wants to do these same things for everyone. We all have the ability that He has given us to shine, just as children do. We are all destined for greatness!!! What holds us back from our blessings are our own selves. We put limits on what God can and will do for us. The same power that He has, we also have. If we only take hold of Gods word and believe it, all things are possible.

My story may not be everyone's story. I don't in any way blame my mother for what happened back then. The enemy was busy doing what He does best. The best part about it is that God is able to get the glory for everything that happened. God had a plan for a breakthrough in my life. My experiences have made me realize that even way back when I was six, God had his hand of my life. He knew what I was going to be even before I was born. What I had to learn was the Lord was only taking me through those situations to make me stronger. Somewhere along the way, I got confused and allowed the enemy to take captive my mind and lead me to believe that God was not there anymore. What I know is the devil is a liar and I know who I am in Christ. I am destined for greatness in the kingdom. God loves me and He loves you too. I am still the same person; I just know and understand that God is real. I am developing a stronger personal relationship with the Lord and that is an exciting feeling. 2 Chronicles 7:14 states "if my people who are called by my name will humble themselves and pray and seek my face and turn from their wicked ways, then will I hear from heaven and will forgive their sin and will heal their land." He is healing me, even as I write. I pray too that He heals you from your past hurts also. I pray that you can learn to embrace your greatness just as I am learning to. Embracing your Greatness is not just a class. Embracing your Greatness is a movement. Women all over the world need to know that they can embrace their greatness. We can be all that God wants us to be and more. The bible says in John 14:12 "He that believeth on me, the works that I do shall he do also; and greater works than these shall he do; because I go unto my Father." Greater works! God has so much in store for His people. If you are going through something, remember that God is going to bring you through it. Be patient, pray, believe and wait on Him. You are destined for greatness!

"You are destined for greatness, designed with a unique purpose, and covered with the anointing of God." — *Dawn M. Harvey*

Putting

God

First

Cassandra Williams- Herbert

There was a time in my walk with Christ where I was saved, but as my mentor say's "I was not submitted to the will of God." I was focusing on making someone else happy. When I gave my life to Christ I knew I did not know anything about being a wife. I was dating a man who I thought that I was going marry. I knew deep down inside that I could not do it without the help of the Lord. I was a babe in Christ and I was just starting to find my way. Even though I knew that I needed Gods help in that relationship, I still attempted to do things my way. What I eventually found out was that God wanted me to do His will for my life and not my own.

One night I came home from a service at church and my boyfriend called me arguing, yet again. He was arguing about something that happened before I got saved. We had broken up before and I had been through so much that I decided to go out one night. I met a nice guy. We began to spend time together. He said all the right things and did all the right things but he seemed too good to be true so I stopped seeing him. I just did not feel like he was sincere. Later my boyfriend and I got back together after he began to show me that he had changed. I never told him about the guy I met when we were apart. Needless, to say he did find out but the story he heard was all wrong. Clearly he heard someone else's version of the truth and of course, he was angry. I tried to explain to him that it happened when we broke up but he didn't want to hear anything I had to say.

Later that night I was awaken by a knock on the window. It was my boyfriend. He told me to let him in. I remember thinking to myself that he looked like a different person. He was acting like he was crazy. I knew I didn't do anything wrong so I figured that he would calm down. After opening the door, he grabbed me and told me that I was lying. Everything happened so fast. Before I knew it I was in the room in the back of my house. I had always thought that I would be safe because my mother and father lived in front of my house and sisters next door. Well, that didn't matter because he began to beat and choke me. He chocked me until my body went limp. I couldn't even cry for help because his hands were so tight around my neck. At that point, I remembered a mother at the church jumping up at prayer meeting and saying prayer changes things. So I began to pray and plead the Blood of Jesus. I began asking God to stop him from beating me. As I prayed the beating stopped. I was able to slowly raise my head and it looked like whatever had control of him was released. It seemed as though he was himself again. Whatever it was that had control of him was gone. I began to feel as if the spirit was saying "you are lucky that you prayed." The sad part is that I forgave him and did not leave him. I actually turned my back on the people that cared about me. My loved ones who saw how bad I was beaten were the ones I became angry with when they told me I needed to leave him. In my mind, I was so sure that this was not his true character and that he must be going through something. I just knew that he was my soul mate. Weeks later I discovered I was pregnant. By then, I had made up in my mind that this was meant to be so I kept the baby and stood by my man.

On August 27, 1996 I gave birth to my son, Cardell. I was so excited that I almost forgot that it was also my birthday. The excitement also numbed the pain from the beating I had endured. It is amazing that one day can be filled with so much joy and have such an undertone of pain. I remember thinking, here I was again, giving birth to my second child and the father was right by side. At least that's what I thought. I thought that I had found my soul mate. Those were the words my grandmother said to me. I can still remember her whisper in my ear. Though we appeared to be in a great relationship to everyone else I was haunted by the abuse. A few days after giving birth, my son's father called and said that he would not be able to bring us home from the hospital because he had to work. I was upset and very sad. I didn't understand how he could just leave us at the hospital. I was his girlfriend and this was his newborn son. This was amazing to me because I felt like he was my soul mate. All I wanted to do was please him. What a big mistake.

By the year 2000, he had begun seeing other women behind my back. I soon realized that when he said he was at work that he was really out cheating on me. On one occasion he was with another female at her family reunion. I became so depressed and overwhelmed after finding out that he was being unfaithful. I found myself trying to figure out why this was happening to me. I felt like I was alone and that he had gone on with his life. I am so blessed that God was with me through this trial. What I discovered was that I was a good woman when he found me and that through it all I was a still a good woman, even if he left. I made a decision to keep my head up no matter what. My deepest fear was that I would not get over him. I feared the loss of this love would leave a space in me that I would never be able to fill. I didn't know what I was going to do without him. He was everything to me. Soon my life began to change because I realized that Jesus was everything. I was tired of all the confusion, disrespect, cheating, abuse, neglect, secrets, lies and the division in our family. I had tried everything and the only thing left to do was pray and ask God to help me.

He answered my prayer. In my willingness to move with God and trust Him for the answer I understand more about myself and my life. The Bible says in 1 Peter 4:12 - 13 "Think it not strange concerning the fiery trail which is to try you; as though some strange thing happen unto you. But rejoice in as much ye are partaking of Christ sufferings; that when his glory shall be revealed, yet may ye be glad also with exceeding joy." I began to understand that there would be some challenges in my life but I have joy knowing that God will be glorified in my life.

I still found myself dealing with the emotions during my process. One day I was at work and I had a break down. I felt something in my spirit asking "Why do you love something that does not love you?" I didn't want to accept that I was with this man for eleven years and he didn't love me. We spent all of our time arguing, analyzing or discussing the relationship. It was time for me to stop taking part in it. At some point you need to ask if this problem is a detour, flat tire or if it is time to get off the highway altogether. It was time for me to get off the highway and find another route to my destiny.

I wanted to become a woman of self-worth, vision and a dreamer. I wanted my desires to be fulfilled. I was constantly making excuses for my life and my future. I know now that I had to be sure about what I wanted out of life. I began to define my goals by writing them down and began seeking God for His will in life, not my own. I knew that this relationship had to end right away. What I realized was that I was the one who was outside the will of God. It was almost as if we feel like we have it all figured out and the plan we have for our life is the right plan. When the truth is, the perfect plan for our life is already in place. I was just in denial. I had to put everything in God's hands. For too long, I allowed my life to be the sum total of all of my decisions. This time I wanted what God wanted for me and my family

After my process of self-discovery, I began to question my prayer life. Did God hear me? Was there a reason that He was not answering me? Was it because of

204 ⋙ *Embracing Our Greatness*

the mistakes that I had made? Were my prayers even getting through? Could He see or feel my pain? Why did it hurt so badly? As I began to work through the practice of getting my life on track with God's help, I have found out over and over again that God would never forget about His children. He knows exactly where and what we are going through. He is aware of every tear that we cry and every step that we take.

One year I took a trip to Sacramento California and Lake Tahoe. It was amazing. By the end of the trip I was refreshed and excited to get back home. I flew back to North Carolina without a care in the world. I felt like this was a beginning and a fresh start for my life. Upon my return my neighbor told me the sheriff had come to my home on several occasions while I was on vacation. I felt like it was just some mistake and that maybe they might have had the wrong address. Just to be sure I went down to the local courthouse to find out what was going on. The clerk asked me if I knew my ex-boyfriend and of course I said yes. Then she told me that she needed to get a deputy. I was totally unprepared for what was about to take place next. I was read my rights and headed to dress out. Dress out is where you change into the orange jail clothes. It was official. I was being arrested for assault with a deadly weapon. I began to explain to the deputy who was arresting me that my ex-boyfriend and I had broken up a few months before and we had an argument then. I remember that when we finished arguing he said that he was going to get me. I had no idea that he would go this far. He had went and told them that I made him feel threatened. He was 6 feet 4 inches tall. How would I have been able to make someone that large feel threatened? He was not threatened, he was angry. All I remember after I finished explaining to the officer what happened was hearing the officer say "You must go through the procedures, but I am going to help you." As I sat there I heard a voice say to me "How many times have I shown you?" And at the minute I knew that God was trying to save me from my own mistakes.

It is only the glory of God that he did not show up for the court date and I was released. The false charges were dropped and it was finally over. The judge just let me go. What I am telling you is I didn't understand why I was in that place or situation then. What I do understand is that God will allow life to get your attention when He has something for you to do for the Kingdom of God. Even though I was praying for

God to release me from this relationship I never imagined that I would ever see the inside of a jail. Today I am thankful for all of my lessons and I praise God for all of His mercy. God promises us that He'll be a shelter in the time of a storm; a way where there seems to be none, a supplier for every need. I stood falsely accused and our Father who is all-powerful freed me.

One of the most important things that you could ever do in your life is love the Lord and love who He created you to be. You have to find happiness within yourself and it's through the love of God that we do this. We cannot allow what someone else does to destroy your life. Why would we allow the actions of another to rob us of our peace and joy? The relationship that I was in had began to control me. I would sit by the telephone hoping that he would call. I would sit by the window and look out every time a car drove by hoping that it was him. I never went out with my friends because I didn't want to miss seeing him. Then one day I woke up. It was like God quickened my spirit. God wanted me to search for Him the way I was searching for this man. It was at that instance that I repented and decided to be obedient. It was time for me to be free. I begin to take my life back. Not leaning on someone else to give me meaning, purpose or happiness. This relationship took me through different stages and I am so grateful for it now. I realized that it was not about pleasing him, it was about pleasing God.

The Bible says: Philippians 4:19 "Paul said... God shall supply all your needs according to his riches and glory by Christ Jesus. My question to you is who can make you whole again? The answer is "Nothing but the blood of Jesus." In retrospect, I now believe that God had shown me all the signs that this was not the man for me. But I found myself really wanting this relationship. I thought that being in a relationship defined who I was. My prayer for you is that you see the signs early. I pray that you do not have to go through what I went through before you realize how much God loves you. Jeremiah 29:11 says for I know the plans I have for you... plans to prosper you and not to harm you, plans to give you hope and a future. The devil will not get the victory in my life. As I began to search myself and what I wanted out of life, things began to change for me. I was a single parent again. And because I was skeptical when I met Mr. Right I lost out on Mr. Wonderful. I was full of pain but I was willing to take the necessary steps to get to my destination.

My life coach Pastor Dawn Harvey stated one night that ministries are birthed out of pain. This would later explain how I was able to move me toward my vision and passion. I am remarried and I have had another child. Isn't God amazing? I have also birthed a women's ministry POW-WOW, Inc. There are so many things that are yet to be birthed and I know that it is just a matter of time. I hope that this encourages you to keep moving even when you make a mistake. What matters is what God says about you. And He says that you are blessed and you will be a blessing.

God's

Divine

Plan

Spotlight Testimony

Chelsea Smith

I am honored to be chosen for a spotlight testimony in this wonderful work of art. My testimony evolves from my experience dealing with the divorce of my parents. I thank God that my steps are divinely orchestrated by Him. Let me tell you about God. He pre-ordained for me to be born at such a time as this. He did not birth me in days of Noah or in the 1700's during the presidency of George Washington. He did not birth me in the 1800's during the tenure of Abraham Lincoln. I thank God. I could have been born during the time of slavery but God did not allow that to happen. He birthed me in the 1900's during the 20th century where Richard Milhous Nixon was the President.

While Nixon, the 37th President of the United States, was in office, God allowed a number of things to happen. There was a lot of warfare in the spirit during this time. There was a crisis in East Pakistan. Countries were fighting just as they are today. It was named the Indo-Pakistan War of 1971. India and Pakistan were shooting explosive bombs at one another to gain rights to territory. Basically, they were fighting over land.

Another event that I can recall was the first sex shops opening for business in 1971. I believe that this was the plan and action of the devil for sex to be sold for profit. Thirty-five years later, in my opinion, sex is still an issue with our country. Films are available for viewing to 18 year olds with R-ratings. These are restricted ratings for viewing. God only wants our eyes on things that honor him. God protects us from this madness by using the scripture "Flee fornication" For every bad thing that the devil tries to throw on us, God makes a way of escape for us from the traps.

The U.S. dollar is devalued for the 2nd time in U.S. History. Everyone needs money. Money cannot create happiness but you need it to survive. With God's provision that was possible. Even though the value was low He was still Jehovah-Jireh in my life. He provided for me and my family. God is so good and His mercy endureth forever.

My mother and father married in 1969 and in 1971 I was born. In 1989, a crisis struck my world. My parents decided to divorce. I moved in with my God parents at that time. I know that God was making a way of escape for me. God knows and will always put you in the right place at the right time. He will make provision for you. He placed me in a loving home, with loving people who were ministers of the Gospel. That was a set up! A divine set up from God. He placed me among people who studied the Word of God and worshiped God in Spirit and in truth. I couldn't ask for anything better than that. I enjoyed my stay with my God parents. It was a place of peace and restoration. I was able to go to my senior prom and graduate from high school with an Advanced Studies Diploma. The only problem I had was the short separation between me and my sister. She lived one place and I lived in another.

I had no clear idea of what I wanted to do after high school. There were so many decisions to be made. What did I want to do with my life? I remember visiting some colleges in the Hampton Roads area with Galilee Baptist Church. We visited one university which was not for me. We visited another state university, definitely not for me. Then we visited Hampton Institute University. This school was so awesome. It had everything that I wanted. It was a little city surrounded by water in the country. Who could ask for more? God does give you the desires of your heart you know. Fancy cars, good-looking guys, girls fashionably dressed to impress, fun atmosphere and a beautiful campus. I decided to apply to Hampton. I really did know if I would get accepted because it was the most prestigious historically black college in America. I always wanted the best in life, so I told myself to go for it. One day I went to the small post office in Warsaw, VA and opened the mailbox. There it was! It was my acceptance letter. I remember I had a big smile on my face as I was reading it. I almost stopped at the congratulations part. But I continued. I got accepted to Hampton University. God was there all the time making the crooked places straight. That's what He did for me.

My spotlight testimony is my determination to not allow what was broken in my parent's life to break the rest of my life. God had a divine plan for my life. Even though my parents divorced, I found myself at a place where only God could help me, yet I kept pressing on. The prize was that He gave me a good life. He blessed me with a life full of relationship with Him. I am not a victim of my circumstances. I am victorious through Christ Jesus over my circumstances.

I truly believe that God loves me. I can just see God running to be with me every day of my life. I was purposed and destined. My desire is to just run out and meet Him. At this moment, I am "Embracing My Greatness." I am in the presence of the lover of my soul, my true love, my eternal escort. The scriptures tell me that "joy comes in the morning." We know that morning is not necessarily in the morning time, but it is when you wake up. You may wake up at six o'clock in the a.m. or eleven o'clock p.m. I visualize it as being whenever you open your eyes up to the Lord and say "Thank You" Right now I am truly living in my morning.

****

A Personal Invitation

I sincerely pray that you have been touched by the words
written on these pages. It is my desire that you have
discovered that there is more to your life than your
current situation. If you do not know the Lord Jesus as
your personal Savior, we invite you to receive Him into
your life. There is nothing like a personal relationship
with Him. I humbly offer you the invitation to accept
Jesus into your heart right now.
The key to salvation is in Romans 10:9-10. It is in your
heart. I know you feel it. You feel the love that surpasses
all understanding. You have never been alone and deep
down in your heart you have always felt it. I believe it is
the love of God that you have felt, unknowingly inside
you all of your lives.   Please accept Him and His
unconditional love. Jesus Christ died for you and He
loves you no matter what your past has said about you.
I offer Christ to you today. Will you accept the
invitation? He is waiting on you to say yes.

~Pastor Dawn M. Harvey

If you have received Jesus as your Lord and Savior or rededicated your life to Him, please contact us. We have a special gift we would like to give to you.

Dawn M. Harvey Ministries, Inc.
5887 Allentown Road
Camp Springs, MD 20746
240-619-3852
www.dawnmharvey.com

Tell Your Story

I pray that you have been changed by the testimonies that you have just read. Still, this book is not complete without the most important story. Your story. The following pages are here so that you can begin your personal testimony and story. Why? I do not just want you to be excited about the move of God our lives; I want you to get excited about the move of God in your life.

Do you believe that you are a survivor? Well I do. Each one of us has a life to live yet somewhere throughout our lives we may have been challenged finding it. I am asking you to illustrate in the next few pages, your process and your deliverance. May the love of God consume and comfort you as you pen away your past and prophecy your future.

"And they overcame him by the blood of the Lamb and
by the word of their testimony."
Revelation 12:11

In His Service,
Pastor Dawn

Tell Your Story

230 ∞ *Embracing Our Greatness*

To order additional copies of:

Embrace Your Greatness, Volume 1

Please contact:

Unlock Publishing House
5887 Allentown Road
Camp Springs, Maryland 20746
240-619-3852

Or visit online at

www.dawnmharvey.com

Email

info@dawnmharvey.com

To request Dawn M. Harvey to speak as a radio/television personality or at your conference, corporate training, women's fellowship, book club or event:

Please contact:

Dawn M. Harvey Ministries, Inc.
5887 Allentown Road
Camp Springs, Maryland 20746
240-619-3852